access to history
themes

The
INDUSTRIALISATION
of BRITAIN
1780–1914

Phil Chapple

Hodder & Stoughton

A MEMBER OF THE HODDER HEADLINE GROUP

Acknowledgements
The publishers would like to thank the following for permission to reproduce material in the volume: Cambridge University Press for extracts from Richard Brown, *Economic Revolution in Britain 1750-1850*, 1992, p. 49 and p. 91 and for an extract from D.S. Landes, *The Unbound Prometheus*, 1976, p. 336; Macmillan for an extract from S.B. Saul, *The Myth of the Great Depression*, 1981, p. 40; Methuen for an extract from W. Ashworth, *An Economic History of England: 1870-1939*, 1981, p. 194; Oxford University Press for an extract from Aspinall and Smith (eds), *English Historical Documents* Vol. XI, pp. 546-7, and for an extract from G.R. Hawke, *Railways and Economic Growth in England and Wales, 1840-1970*, 1970, p. 59; Penguin for an extract from Karl Marx and Friedrich Engels, *The Communist Manifesto*, 1985, p. 87.

The publishers would like to thank the following for permission to reproduce copyright illustrations in this volume: The pictures on pages 65 and 80 are reproduced courtesy of *Punch*.

Every effort has been made to trace and acknowledge ownership of copyright. The publishers will be glad to make any suitable arrangements with copyright holders whom it has not been possible to contact.

Orders: please contact Bookpoint Ltd, 39 Milton Park, Abingdon, Oxon OX14 4TD. Telephone: (44) 01235 400414, Fax: (44) 01235 400454. Lines are open from 9.00 - 6.00, Monday to Saturday, with a 24 hour message answering service. Email address: orders@bookpoint.co.uk

British Library Cataloguing in Publication Data

A catalogue for this title is available from the British Library

ISBN 0 340 72069 7

First published 1999

Impression number	10	9	8	7	6	5	4	3	2	1	
Year			2005	2004	2003	2002	2001	2000		1999	

The cover picture is entitled 'Industry on the Tyne' by William Bell-Scott (1861), Wallington Hall, Northumberland, reproduced courtesy of the Bridgeman Art Library.

Typeset by Sempringham publishing services, Bedford
Printed in Great Britain for Hodder & Stoughton Educational,
a division of Hodder Headline Plc, 338 Euston Road, London NW1 3BH
by Redwood Books, Trowbridge, Wiltshire.

Contents

Preface

The original *Access to History* series was conceived as a collection of sets of books covering popular chronological periods in British history, such as 'the Tudors' and 'the nineteenth century', together with the histories of other countries, such as France, Germany, Russia and the USA. This arrangement complemented the way in which early modern and modern history has traditionally been taught in sixth forms, colleges and universities. In recent years, however, other ways of dividing up the past have become increasingly popular. In particular, there has been a greater emphasis on studying relatively brief periods in considerable detail and on comparing similar historical phenomena in different countries. These developments have generated a demand for appropriate learning materials, and, in response, two new 'strands' are being added to the main series - *In Depth* and *Themes*. The new volumes build directly on the features that have made *Access to History* so popular.

To the general reader

Although *Access* books have been specifically designed to meet the needs of examination students, these volumes also have much to offer the general reader. *Access* authors are committed to the belief that good history must not only be accurate, up-to-date and scholarly, but also clearly and attractively written. The main body of the text (excluding the 'Study Guides') should, therefore, form a readable and engaging survey of a topic. Moreover, each author has aimed not merely to provide as clear an explanation as possible of what happened in the past but also to stimulate readers and to challenge them into thinking for themselves about the past and its significance. Thus, although no prior knowledge is expected from the reader, he or she is treated as an intelligent and thinking person throughout. The author tends to share ideas and explore possibilities, instead of delivering so-called 'historical truths' from on high.

To the student reader

It is intended that *Access* books should be used by students studying history at a higher level. Its volumes are all designed to be working texts, which should be reasonably clear on a first reading but which will benefit from re-reading and close study. To be an effective and successful student, you need to budget your time wisely. Hence you should think carefully about how important the material in a particular book is for you. If you simply need to acquire a general grasp of a topic, the following approach will probably be effective:

I. Read Chapter 1, which should give you an overview of the whole book, and think about its contents.

2. Skim through Chapter 2, paying particular attention to the opening section and to the headings and sub-headings. Decide if you need to read the whole chapter.
3. If you do, read the chapter, stopping at the end of every sub-division of the text to make notes.
4. Repeat stage 2 (and stage 3 where appropriate) for the other chapters.

If, however, your course - and your particular approach to it - demands a detailed knowledge of the contents of the book, you will need to be correspondingly more thorough. There is no perfect way of studying, and it is particularly worthwhile experimenting with different styles of note-making to find the one that best suits you. Nevertheless, the following plan of action is worth trying:

1. Read a whole chapter quickly, preferably at one sitting. Avoid the temptation - which may be very great - to make notes at this stage.
2. Study the flow diagram at the end of the chapter, ensuring that you understand the general 'shape' of what you have read.
3. Re-read the chapter more slowly, this time taking notes. You may well be amazed at how much more intelligible and straightforward the material seems on a second reading - and your notes will be correspondingly more useful to you when you have to write an essay or revise for an exam. In the long run, reading a chapter twice can, in fact, often save time. Be sure to make your notes in a clear, orderly fashion, and spread them out so that, if necessary, you can later add extra information.
4. Read the advice on essay questions, and do tackle the specimen titles. (Remember that if learning is to be effective, it must be active. No one - alas - has yet devised any substitute for real effort. It is up to you to make up your own mind on the key issues in any topic.)
5. Attempt the source-based questions. The guidance on tackling these exercises, which is generally given at least once in a book, is well worth reading and thinking about.

When you have finished the main chapters, go through the 'Further Reading' section. Remember that no single book can ever do more than introduce a topic, and it is to be hoped that - time permitting - you will want to read more widely. If *Access* books help you to discover just how diverse and fascinating the human past can be, the series will have succeeded in its aim - and you will experience that enthusiasm for the subject which, along with efficient learning, is the hallmark of all the best students.

Robert Pearce

1 Introduction: British Industrialisation

The industrialisation of Britain is arguably the most significant development in the modern history of the nation. An economy and people largely dependent upon the land were transformed into the world's first industrial economy and society in little over a century. This process of industrialisation accelerated from the 1780s during the era which has become popularly (if not strictly accurately) referred to as the industrial revolution. One of the greatest scholars of British industrialisation, E.J. Hobsbawm, considered this era as 'the most fundamental transformation of human life in the history of the world recorded in written documents'.[1]

The period c. 1780-1914 was thus one of immense long-term change in the economic fortunes of the country. This change manifested itself in a variety of ways, the most important of which was the rise of manufacturing industry. This involved major structural change in the economy with the emphasis shifting away from traditional sectors such as agriculture towards manufacturing industry and mining. In some industrial sectors, most notably cotton textiles, old forms of production and organisation were swept away as new technologies and non-manual sources of power superseded production in the home. In cotton textiles the industrial revolution ushered in the age of the factory, where the widespread adoption of first water and then steam power drove the new cotton mills. The British coal industry too expanded rapidly, to fuel the new iron foundries and steam engines. However, industrialisation was about much more than industry. Agriculture, domestic and foreign trade, banking and finance, transport, construction, population growth and the expansion of empire were all part of this process. All are addressed to varying degrees in this book.

Historians have struggled to fully explain this phenomenon of industrialisation since it first attracted the serious attention of scholars from the late nineteenth century. Since then economic historians have utilised a vast range of sources, especially statistical evidence, in the search for an understanding of why Britain became the world's first industrial nation. However, restricting oneself to statistical sources can cloud some of the more human issues associated with industrialisation. Whilst this book will provide an overview of the economic aspects of industrialisation, students must be aware of the human aspect. The response of individuals to economic opportunities was a driving force behind industrialisation. Arkwright, Darby, Watt, Boulton and Wedgwood are all familiar names of the period: individually, and collectively perhaps, they demonstrate the inventive and innovative spirit of the age. Yet the unknown millions, including textile operatives, labourers, coal miners, farmers and merchants, were all part of the industrialisation process. They were part of what became a revolution in the human experience. This may have been a transformation that took over 100 years to happen, a point that has prompted many historians to talk of 'evolution'; but in the context of the long recorded history of mankind a century is a very short time indeed and therefore many agree that a 'revolution' did occur. Historians have long debated the impact of industrialisation on the lives of the people. The pessimistic view, promoted by historians in the 1960s and 1970s such as E.P. Thompson and E.J. Hobsbawm, focussed upon the negative aspects of industrialisation. The exploitation of labour, degenerating urban conditions and an overall decline in the quality of life formed the basis of the pessimists' view. Optimists, including T.S. Ashton and R.G. Hartwell pointed to the fact that industrialisation created millions of jobs for an expanding population. This is a debate which continues. Whatever one's view on this issue, the economic, social, political, cultural and ecological consequences of industrialisation have fundamentally altered the world. That process began in Britain in the eighteenth century.

1 Industrial Revolution

It is impossible for historians to give precise dates for the industrial revolution. It is generally accepted that, after the 1770s, a more dynamic economic performance in specific sectors pushed the economy into a new phase of economic growth. The acceleration of this growth from the 1780s represents the start of a period which has since been dubbed the 'industrial revolution'. Deciding at which point the industrial revolution ended is equally problematic. Traditionally, the dominant view has been that by the 1830s the revolution was over and that, thereafter, the railway-building era and the creation of Britain as a free-trade nation represented a new phase of growth. Yet this view is not without its detractors, with some historians referring to an industrial revolution after 1830. Whichever view we subscribe to, one fundamental truth remains. Unlike the suddenness with which, for example, a political revolution usually takes place, the British industrial revolution was at least 50 years and possibly more in the making.

The first use of the term is generally credited to the French economist Blanqui in 1837. He believed that the changes taking place in Britain were as significant as the French political revolution of 1789. The theme of revolution was also pursued by the German socialist and close political associate of Marx, Friedrich Engels, who in 1844 had referred to the steam engine and cotton textile inventions as giving rise to an industrial revolution. The phrase was popularised in Britain following Arnold Toynbee's *Lectures on the Industrial Revolution* of 1884. Popular as the title has become, however, its validity remains as controversial as ever. Any change which affected society in so many more ways than the simply industrial requires a title that also acknowledges the broader impact of this change.

So how revolutionary was the industrial revolution? The early historians of the industrial revolution were in no doubt of the revolutionary impact. Beard claimed in 1901 that, 'England of the first part of the eighteenth century was virtually a medieval England, quiet, primeval and undisturbed by the roar of trade and commerce. Suddenly, almost like a thunderbolt from a clear sky, were ushered in the storm and stress of the industrial revolution.'[2] Few today subscribe to this cataclysmic interpretation of events, as historians emphasise the gradual nature of change. Indeed, since J.H. Clapham's influential three-volumed *Economic History of Modern Britain* was published between 1826 and 1938, the term industrial revolution has been used to identify a period of history rather than indicate an accepted view of events. Current historical opinion places greater emphasis on the idea of accelerated levels of growth over decades. What is clear is that by the beginning of the Victorian period the country had changed fundamentally from the Britain of 60 or so years before. It was the extent of change, relative to previous generations, that made this period unique.

Although the industrial revolution took over 50 years to happen the title itself resolutely refuses to die. It has been extremely durable, arguably because no acceptable substitute has been offered. The term does, at least, capture the significance of the age even if 'industrial' is too specific and 'revolutionary' remains questionable. As Mokyr explains, 'Economic historians, like all scholars, need certain terms and concepts with which they can conduct their discourse, even if arguments about the *precise* definitions of these concepts continue … It is hard to argue that the concept should be abandoned, for the simple reason that scholars feel that it communicates and insist on using it.'[3]

What then should the concept of industrial revolution convey? It signifies more than the increased adoption of new technologies in manufacturing and mining or a rapid increase in output levels, as important as they were. The emergence of a more complex and more modern economy, the beginning of a revolution in transport and communications, the transformation of agriculture and its role in the new society are all interrelated parts of this phenomenon. So too are the social and political changes which resulted from industrialisation.

2 The Physical Aspects of Change

Britain in 1914 was a vastly different place when compared to the late eighteenth century. The transformation of Britain was particularly significant in terms of the physical changes which affected all parts of the kingdom, albeit to varying degrees. The most striking aspect of this change was demographic, i.e. related to population. The steady growth of the eighteenth century, which had seen the population of

Great Britain (excluding Ireland) double from five to ten million, became a population explosion in the following century. An average growth in numbers of over 15 per cent per decade saw the nation's population reach almost 41 million at the outbreak of the First World War. The major result of this growth was the urbanisation of Britain, as a greater proportion of the population came to live in urban rather than rural areas, as we see in the bar chart below.

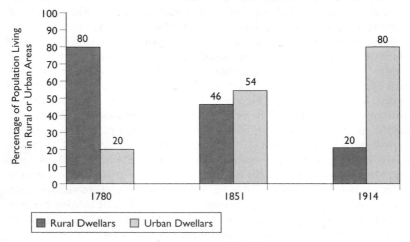

Urbanisation, 1780-1914

Understandably, the most significant growth occurred in the developing towns and cities associated with industrialisation. As industrialisation progressed, the growth of the great industrial cities on the coalfields continued accordingly. With the increased use of coal for

Growth of selected towns and cities, 1801-1901			
Town	Population 1801	Population 1901	Percentage Increase
Birmingham	71,000	760,000	970
Bolton	18,000	168,000	833
Bradford	13,000	280,000	2,053
Bristol	61,000	329,000	439
Glasgow	77,000	904,000	1,081
Halifax	12,000	105,000	775
Liverpool	82,000	685,000	735
Manchester	75,000	645,000	760
Sheffield	46,000	381,000	728

the generation of steam power and for use as a direct source of heat for industrial processes such as iron or brick production, urbanisation became concentrated in areas with immediate access to coal. Thus emerged the great industrial regions, most notably in northern England, the Midlands, the central lowlands of Scotland and in South Wales. Away from the coalfields, the ports which served the industrial areas, such as Liverpool, also experienced significant expansion. Indeed, almost if not all towns in Britain experienced some degree of population growth as part of a general trend. In the industrial centres, however, such growth was particularly marked.

The combination of industry and rapid population growth created the typical industrial landscape. Coal mines, iron foundries and cotton textile mills set against a backdrop of terraced streets became the most enduring image of industrialisation. Yet, as accurate a picture that this might be, there were also countless settlements, often with a population of no more than a few hundred, existing on the employment of a single mill or pit. In some of the more remote areas of the kingdom, however, the physical effects of industrialisation were barely apparent until the latter decades of the nineteenth century. Much of Scotland, Wales and parts of England remained isolated until the arrival of the railway, and in extreme cases the motor car. This too was the reality of industrialisation. Nevertheless, the dynamic expansion of ports and coalfield-based industrial centres dominated the nineteenth century and it is in these areas that the future of the industrial nation was defined.

3 The Economic Transformation of Britain

A brief and essentially general survey of our period suggests that fundamental and wide-ranging economic change occurred. There are a number of clearly identifiable sectors of the economy which remain central to this story of industrialisation. These include the emergence of a narrow, though hugely important, industrial base, which included both manufacturing and mining. Secondly, a transport revolution took place with remarkable economic and social results, allowing the opening up of domestic and foreign markets and facilitating greater personal travel. Thirdly, we must also recognise the changing nature of the British economy and the increasingly important part played by entrepreneurs, i.e. those individuals whose managerial skills and willingness to invest in industrial ventures created the factories, mines and workshops associated with industrialisation. Finally, we must bear in mind the fortunes of agriculture and the place it came to occupy in industrialising Britain.

a) Manufacturing and Mining

The importance of manufacturing and mining to the economy is central to the process of industrialisation, as the share of national

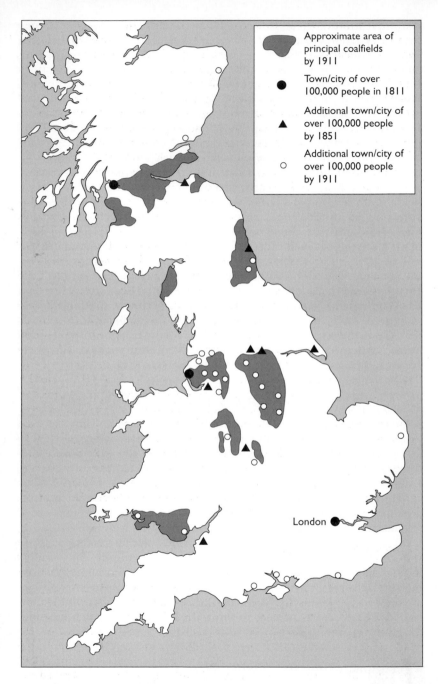

Principal coalfields of Britain and towns and cities with a population over 100,000 between 1811 and 1911

income from the two sectors rose from 16 per cent in 1760 to 23 per cent in 1801 and 40 per cent a century later. It is surprising perhaps just how precariously narrow the industrial base actually was, relying as it did on the three 'staple' industries of textiles: iron and steel and coal. The growing dominance of cotton textiles is one of the more remarkable aspects of the early period of industrialisation. As a proportion of total value of exports, for example, cotton textiles accounted for just 2.3 per cent in 1790. Yet by the start of the 1830s, the figure had risen to almost 60 per cent. A huge increase in demand and an ability to maximise the potential of new technologies to meet that demand had propelled cotton textiles beyond the more traditional woollen industry as the dominant textile sector.

The coal and iron and steel industries were the only other industrial sectors in the earlier stages of industrialisation to make a significant break with the traditional small-scale workshop or pit. Other sectors such as brewing, pottery and brickmaking did produce some examples of larger-scale organisations, though these were the exception rather than the rule. Keeping this change in perspective is of course important, and there were, within the cotton, iron and steel and coal sectors, many remaining examples of small-scale operations. Nevertheless, these sectors dominated the industrial scene for most of the nineteenth century. Production levels in the staples rose consistently, though by the mid century this was accompanied by the emergence of a broader industrial base through the development of the engineering sector in particular. Machine-making, shipbuilding and a range of products associated with the railway industry reduced the economy's dependence on the 'staple' industries of cotton, coal and iron. Technological advance in the mid century, especially in steam generation and propulsion and in the production of high quality cheap steel, enhanced Britain's industrial prospects and reaffirmed the importance of manufacturing. The scale of industrial expansion after the industrial revolution should not be underestimated. The growth too of the industrial centres was considerably greater than in the industrial revolution (1780s-1830s) period.

b) Transport Revolution

Industrialisation on the scale achieved would not have been possible without essential improvements in transport facilities. Improvements in the transport of freight, especially of bulky raw materials such as coal, lay at the heart of improved industrial performance. Similarly, the transport of finished items to markets both at home and to the ports of shipment abroad was radically improved from the latter stages of the eighteenth century onwards. Between 1760 and 1820 over £20 million was invested in canal building in Britain. The result was a 4,000 mile network of canals linking the major ports, cities and industrial centres.

An 18,000-mile rail network, constructed from 1830 and largely completed by the 1880s, superseded canals. The 'Railway Age' contributed to a second phase of the transport revolution. As congestion increased on key parts of the canal network and as some canal companies exploited their monopoly by charging excessive tolls, so an alternative was sought. Railways provided that alternative. The railway's direct contribution to improving and speeding up delivery, whilst cutting costs and also providing opportunity for personal travel, radically affected the economy and society. Transport had become a crucial aspect of business and in doing so further enhanced Britain's economic power, a fact that was reinforced by developments in ocean-going transport in the second half of the nineteenth century.

c) Economic Policy and Industrialisation

In the late eighteenth century a number of restrictions existed which affected Britain's trade with the rest of the world. In order to raise funds for central government, the State enforced duties on most imports. The duties charged on the principal imports of foodstuffs, industrial raw materials and luxury goods such as tobacco and wines were an important source of income for government in the absence of income tax. Further restrictions existed on the export of certain machine products and even on the migration of some skilled craftsmen, in order to stop foreign competitors benefiting from British expertise. Furthermore, the Navigation Laws (see page 46), first implemented in the seventeenth century, ensured that British ships carried goods to and from British ports.

The idea that such intervention in trade by government might actually be harmful to British economic development (a theme explored in detail in Chapter 3) was first effectively articulated in Adam Smith's *Wealth of Nations* in 1776. This highly influential work popularised the idea that a *laissez-faire* economic policy, involving freedom from government involvement, would encourage growth and prosperity. From this point there began a long process of debate and persuasion which resulted in the eventual removal of almost all trade restrictions by the 1850s. Even before that decade, however, the government had actually played a limited role in the economy or industrialisation. The industrial revolution was not planned. It resulted from the exploitation of favourable economic conditions and opportunities by businessmen. From the 1840s onwards this non-interventionist, or *laissez faire*, policy became the prevailing economic philosophy of successive British governments until the First World War. The 'natural laws' of economics increasingly determined production, prices and wages. Government intervention in the economy became restricted to some regulation of working conditions, such as setting the minimum age at which a child could begin work, the regulation of the length of the working day and the removal of women and children from underground working in Britain's mines. Such social legislation had relatively little impact upon the economic fortunes of industry. Even when British industry was perceived to be falling behind her competitors, such as the United States and Germany, in the last quarter of the nineteenth century, it was not considered appropriate by the majority of businessmen for government to intervene. Even when the American and German governments created tariffs against British imports to protect their own industries from British goods, Britain remained a 'Free Trade' nation.

d) Agriculture

The fortunes of agriculture during the industrial revolution and after were determined by forces at work both on the land and in the wider economy. From the mid-eighteenth century until 1815, the agricultural sector had changed significantly. Population growth boosted demand for food. Coupled with this, the high prices due to war-time inflation during the Napoleonic wars of 1793-1815 served to encourage investment in agriculture as profits rose. The old open-field system, in which open fields of land were divided into strips, and worked by the majority of villagers, gave way to a more productive system of farming whereby the open fields were enclosed. The new enclosed farms allowed for the widespread adoption of more scientific farming, including crop rotation, the draining of previously poor quality land and some, albeit limited, application of machinery. In the pastoral (animal) sector, more scientific breeding programmes improved the quality of livestock. On the larger farms, where more innovative farmers could apply such techniques, significant improvements in profits were often achieved. This in turn encouraged further investment. However, whereas outside forces which boosted prices assisted farming before 1815, so such forces conspired to work against the industry from 1815 until the mid century. The collapse of high war-time prices had a devastating effect in the arable areas, cutting profits, reducing wages and forcing hundreds of thousands of agricultural labourers to emigrate over the following three decades. From the mid century, however, the general prosperity enjoyed in industry was mirrored in agriculture, with a return to buoyant prices, growing demand through population growth and wage improvements. The 'Golden Age' of agriculture was to continue until the final quarter of the century when, for the first time, foreign competition swamped the British market with grain too cheap for most home producers.

The fortunes of agriculture, assessed throughout this book, should therefore be seen in the context of general economic change rather than in isolation. Inevitably, as industry prospered, so the proportion of the workforce employed in the agricultural sector declined relative to that in the industrial sector. This trend is also apparent in the following table highlighting the relative contributions of key sectors of the economy to national income. This does not represent an overall decline in production levels in agriculture. It does, however, demonstrate how the British economy was moving from a predominantly agricultural state to an industrial one.

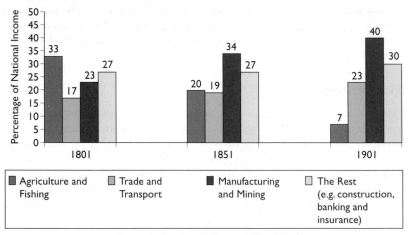

Sources of national income 1801-1901

4 Britain as a World Economic Force

Whilst the home market continued to consume the great bulk of new manufactures, the growth of overseas markets ensured that the rapid growth in production could be sustained, particularly for the cotton-textile sector. The unprecedented economic strength of Britain in the 1780-1914 period was a direct result of the success of her industries in exploiting new markets for her manufactures and in the growing demand in Britain for industrial raw materials and food-stuffs. Even before the industrial revolution, overseas trade had been expanding steadily, with Britain establishing herself as a major trading nation. In particular, the African slave trade, had, from the late seventeenth century, proved to be extremely lucrative. Merchants, especially in Bristol, Liverpool and London, exploited the economic potential of the 'Triangular Trade'. This involved the exchange of British manufactures, such as metal products and weaponry, for human cargoes on the West Coast of Africa. The sale of slaves to the plantation owners of the West Indies or southern states of North America allowed traders to buy plantation products. The profits earned in Britain and Europe from these products, such as tobacco, raw cotton and sugar, helped establish British merchants in international trade. This trade had its moral critics and was eventually eradicated, beginning with the prohibition of the carrying of slaves on British ships in 1807. In 1833 the Emancipation of Slaves

Act made it illegal to keep slaves in British colonies. European trade links, long established, also grew stronger with the general expansion of trade throughout the eighteenth century. Thus, when the pace of industrial activity accelerated and merchants sought overseas markets and products, the British were already in a position to strengthen existing links and develop new trade. As the bar chart below suggests, overseas trade was itself a very significant aspect of the growth of British economy for over 200 years, particularly in the decade after the industrial revolution period.

The continued geographical spread of British overseas trade after the Napoleonic wars demonstrates the extent to which British merchants and manufacturers had infiltrated markets worldwide. Regions as diverse as North and South America, Asia (especially India), Europe and the Middle East and Mediterranean were all part of the trading network which Britain came to dominate. By 1830, 45 per cent of international trade was conducted by the British. The economic prosperity of Britain became increasingly dependent upon her ability to trade. Hundreds of thousands of manufacturing jobs relied upon it, and the nation's ability to feed its citizens increasingly rested on unfettered access to overseas sources of food.

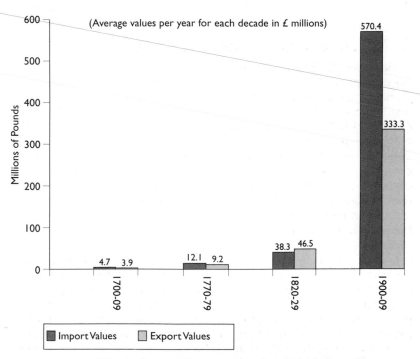

Official values of imports and exports, 1700-1909
(Average values per year for each decade in £ millions)

Territorial acquisitions in the form of empire were inextricably associated with the economic well-being of Britain. Overseas territories provided markets, raw materials and, in some cases, strategic military advantages. The expansion of the British Empire from the industrial revolution to the end of the nineteenth century provided immense economic opportunities. The impact of British colonisation on the indigenous populations remained of secondary importance to British manufacturers, merchants and workers as their livelihoods were so closely linked to colonial markets and suppliers. British colonial possession and trade links on every continent thus reinforced the power and economic influence of the first industrial nation.

However, despite the wealth and power which trade and industry had created, the loss of supremacy in the late nineteenth century was inevitable, as other nations industrialised, and eventually challenged or even surpassed Britain. The damage inflicted upon her economy by the First World War was a critical blow to the nation that had changed the face of the world. The psychological shock of this fall from supremacy was almost as great.

The British economy thus experienced a fundamental transition from 1780 to 1914, and this book aims to enable students to develop a general understanding of the nature, causes and effects of that change.

References

1   E.J. Hobsbawm, *Industry and Empire* (Penguin, 1969), p. 13.
2   C. Beard, *The Industrial Revolution* (Allen & Unwin, 1901), p. 23.
3   J. Mokyr (ed), *The British Industrial Revolution* (Westview, 1993), p. 2.

Summary Diagram
British Industrialisation

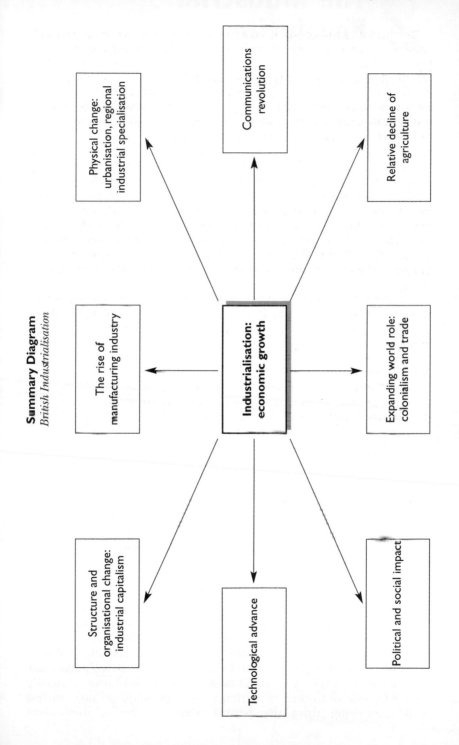

- Physical change: urbanisation, regional industrial specialisation
- Communications revolution
- Relative decline of agriculture
- The rise of manufacturing industry
- Industrialisation: economic growth
- Expanding world role: colonialism and trade
- Structure and organisational change: industrial capitalism
- Technological advance
- Political and social impact

2 The Industrial Revolution

1 Problems and Definitions

To the student unfamiliar with more recent studies, the phrase 'industrial revolution' may still evoke the traditional imagery of an industrial environment. The factory, foundry, mine and the all-pervading influence of the steam engine have erroneously dominated popular perceptions of early industrialisation for too long. However, actually identifying the factors which constitute an industrial revolution is both complex and open to individual interpretation. A useful starting point, offering general guidelines, comes from the economic historian Phyllis Deane, who identified a number of structural changes which, in her view, when taken together, constituted an industrial revolution. For Deane such changes would involve:

i)   The application of new scientific and technical knowledge in industry.

ii)   The development of more specialised industrial firms whose markets were increasingly national or international rather than local.

iii) The growth of industrial towns, and increasing migration from rural areas to urban centres.

iv)   The relative decline in importance of primary industries such as agriculture in favour of manufacturing or service industries.

v)   The growth of large-scale places of employment such as the factory or foundry.

vi)   The widespread substitution of machinery for people in the provision of power or in the production process.

vii) The emergence of a new social order, based on industrialisation, involving the increased economic and political power of the middle class. This would result in the decline in influence of the landed classes.

Such interpretations are a useful starting point in understanding what happened in Britain in the late eighteenth and early nineteenth centuries. However, as we shall see, such changes were not confined to the industrial revolution - far from it! We should also see the industrialisation of Britain in terms of broader change, incorporating developments in economic areas such as investment levels, total production levels, productivity (i.e. output per worker) and other less visible changes. This is not such an easy task, as economic historians rarely enjoy the benefit of easily recognisable 'events' which usually mark political revolutions. The lack of reliable statistics relating to business generally, and industry in particular, makes our task more complex. The small scale of most businesses, usually owned by one individual or perhaps a partnership, resulted in few details surviving from the period. Census returns, themselves relatively unreliable until the mid nineteenth century, help us assess general factors such as population growth, employment patterns and urbanisation. However, they tell us little of specific industrial activity. Other official sources such as government statistics on trade, land ownership and taxation may tell us something of the general economic climate. Crucially, however, statistical sources alone cannot answer the key questions. Why did economic growth accelerate in the last quarter of the eighteenth century? Why did growth accelerate even further after 1815? Why did certain industries enjoy more dramatic growth than others? Do the changes which occurred consti-tute a watershed - or revolution - in the history of the nation? Did agriculture experience a revolution? We are forced to rely upon frag-mentary evidence from many sources to provide possible answers. Economic historians have long addressed these questions regarding the industrial revolution era and yet we still do not actually know for certain why the British economy developed as it did.

2 The 'Traditional' Economy

The industrial revolution did not mark the beginning of industry in Britain. Thus, the economy of the first half of the eighteenth century should not be referred to as a pre-industrial economy, as Britain possessed a relatively successful and skilled industrial sector before the industrial revolution. It follows that manufacturing industry was not a creation of the industrial revolution. Considerable wealth was generated by the textile, metal and coal industries, employing tens of thousands of workers well before the last quarter of the eighteenth century. Some recent estimates suggest that as early as 1700 up to a third of the working population were employed in some form of manufacturing. The slow though steady growth in these sectors, often based in rural areas as well as the towns, has been referred to as a period of 'proto-industrialisation'. Historians have suggested charac-teristics of the economy before the 1780s which distinguish it from the industrial revolution. Rural population predominated, often combining agricultural employment with some manufacturing, particularly in textiles. Low levels of technology were employed in what was primarily domestic industry, and manufacturing growth rates remained low, typically below 1 per cent per annum. Communications remained poor and production was essentially aimed at a local market, with little personal travel for most people outside their immediate locality.

Nevertheless, there still existed a range of industrial enterprises which were to provide the base for future industrial growth. Textiles in particular accounted for a sizeable share of manufacturing output. The woollen industry, concentrated in East Anglia, the West Country and the West Riding of Yorkshire, had a long history of capitalist organisation whereby textile entrepreneurs known as clothiers would control all stages of the 'putting-out' or 'domestic' system, from the purchase of the raw material to the sale of finished cloth at regional woollen markets. They organised production, employing local workers who worked in their own homes. Defoe's description of the Halifax area from his work *A Tour Through the Whole Island of Great Britain 1724-6* indicates a town active in the textile trade. '... This whole country ... is yet infinitely full of people; those people are full of business. The business is the clothing trade ... we could see that almost at every house there was a tenter [a frame used for drying and stretching woollen cloth], and at almost every tenter, a piece of cloth ...'[1] Families involved in the production processes, such as spinning, weaving and finishing, were dependent upon individual clothiers, often renting the spinning wheels or handlooms used in the production of woollen cloth. Wool remained the most important textile industry in terms of output and exports until the end of the Napoleonic wars, by which time two-thirds of the industry's production was centred in the West Riding. Linen and silk also experienced significant growth in the pre-industrial revolution period, with silk production quadrupling between 1720 and 1775. Linen production thrived in parts of Scotland, Ireland and north-west England. Cotton textiles on the other hand remained a minor offshoot of textiles concentrated around south Lancashire, accounting for only 1 per cent of manufacturing output by value in 1770, compared to 8 per cent for silk.

Coal too enjoyed a period of growth, providing essential heat for the increasing number of households and industries such as brewing, glass making and metal smelting, especially by blacksmiths. Coal output trebled between 1700 and 1775 with the growth of coalfields across the country. The metal trades too constituted an important part of the pre-industrial revolution economy where non-ferrous metals, especially lead, copper and tin, made an important contribution to life in some remote areas such as the tin industry in Cornwall, copper in South Wales and lead in the north Pennines. The iron industry thrived in the Sussex Weald, Forest of Dean and the Black Country of the West Midlands. It was in the Black Country, well before the industrial revolution, that a critical innovation occurred when, as early as 1709, Abraham Darby of Coalbrookdale mastered the process of using coke rather than charcoal to smelt iron. A flourishing hardware industry in the West Midlands and cutlery industry in Sheffield had established the industrial credentials of such areas long before the acceleration in growth in the later eighteenth century. Thus textiles and metal goods established themselves as significant industrial sectors, even developing profitable overseas markets as British exports doubled in value in the first half of the century. Leather goods, brewing, pottery, glass and shipbuilding amongst others also made their contribution to a growing manufacturing sector, and it is in the context of this existing industrial base that we should assess future industrial growth. Later growth may have been so dramatic as to eclipse the achievements of the earlier eighteenth century, but we must not overlook the existence of a capitalist industrial sector before the 1770s.

3 The Causes of Accelerated Economic Growth

The industrial revolution, then, is largely a matter of the economy moving into a higher gear. Exactly when this happened is not clear, though by the 1780s there were many signs that the economy was entering a phase of generally accelerated growth. Although modest by today's standards, growth rates rose significantly from the estimated 0.7 per cent per annum average in the first three quarters of the eighteenth century. Recent estimates calculate that growth in the total output of the British economy increased to an annual average rate of 1.3 per cent in the 1780s, rising to around 2 per cent at the turn of the century and accelerating to over 3 per cent by 1830. To contemporaries, the immediate impact of this accelerated growth may have been less apparent than the term 'industrial revolution' would suggest. At various points, war, high food prices, political repression and demands for political reform were the more pressing and immediate issues affecting the population throughout these years, not an awareness of the creation of a new economic order. Nevertheless over the course of a generation the path of history had changed, and the economic, social and political repercussions were to be immense.

What explanations exist for this transformation? For over half a century this has proven to be a most keenly debated question. The short answer is that we do not know. But we do know that it was not planned. There was no strategy to industrialise, no government policy to encourage industrialisation. No single factor can be held responsible and we must accept that the question 'what caused the industrial revolution?' is one which has no specific answer. It is more useful to ask what factors contributed to the acceleration in growth rates from the late eighteenth century and why this growth was sustained thereafter, to the point that, by the third quarter of the nineteenth century, Britain had become the world's 'first industrial nation'.

a) Increasing Domestic Demand

For any industry to thrive it must have a strong demand for its product. In late eighteenth-century Britain an increase in the rate of population growth provided such a stimulus to demand, particularly for the relatively basic necessities of clothing, housing, fuel, food and simple domestic commodities. A relatively slow population growth gave way to rapid acceleration in total numbers in the last third of the eighteenth century as indicated in the bar chart over leaf.

By previous standards this constituted a veritable population

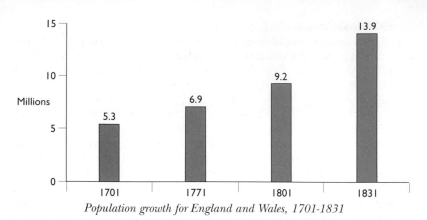

Population growth for England and Wales, 1701-1831

explosion. The explanations for this phenomenon are many and varied, although all revolve around the critical relationship between death rates and birth rates. The period saw a significant decline in annual death rates, estimated at 28 per thousand in 1780 but falling to 21 per thousand in 1830. The principal causes of this declining death rate include the absence of major epidemics of diseases such as typhus, plague or smallpox. There may also have been some increase in real incomes, reflected in increased consumption, particularly in the form of improved diet. Agricultural improvement and transport developments ensured that the growing population could be fed. The increasing birth rate, on the other hand, has been variously explained by the declining average age of marriage, which fell from 28 years of age for men in 1750 to 26 years in 1830. For women, the average age over the same period fell from 27 to 24, and the proportion of women who never married fell from 15 per cent to 7.5 per cent. The employment opportunities presented by economic growth allowed economic independence at an earlier age and may therefore have encouraged earlier marriage. Whatever the underlying causes of population growth, its impact on economic activity was of great significance. Not only were there many more consumers, stimulating demand for a range of products, but also population growth provided a large pool of readily available, relatively cheap labour. Low-wage costs helped keep prices of British manufactures low, further stimulating demand at home and abroad.

b) Technological Advance and Innovation

The value of Britain's stock of industrial buildings and machinery multiplied eightfold during the industrial revolution era. Early studies attributed much of this increase to the rapid expansion in the use of new technology. We now know that such studies tended to exaggerate the technological achievements of the era, recognising today that much of the new machinery was rudimentary and restricted to a few exceptional sectors such as cotton textiles, iron and steam technology.

i) Textile machinery

The single most impressive achievement in the creation of new techniques and their commercial exploitation lies in cotton textiles. As a minor component of the textile industry in the mid eighteenth century, cotton textiles experienced the most revolutionary transformation of any industry. Indeed in many ways the industry exemplified the revolution itself, with cotton masters at the forefront of technological advance and innovation.

Ironically, the technological changes which did occur might easily have been adopted by the woollen industry. Yet the two key elements of spinning and weaving were initially transformed in cotton, as the woollen-textile industry lagged behind, conservatively resisting change. Centred on south Lancashire initially, cotton spinning was the first to embrace new technology. The most important advances are outlined below:

1733, John Kay's 'flying shuttle' (Weaving)

The flying shuttle speeded up the weaving process by moving the shuttle across the loom automatically, rather than the weaver threading it by hand. Although designed to be used in the woollen industry, the shuttle was, in the long term, to influence the cotton sector greatly. The shuttle did not come into widespread use until the mid century, as handloom weavers resisted its introduction, fearing that by speeding up the weaving process, fewer weavers would be needed. As a result, weavers, who feared for their livelihoods, attacked Kay's home in 1753, forcing him to flee the country. The flying shuttle was used on domestic handlooms and did not, therefore, create a demand for textile factories to replace domestic production.

1764, James Hargreaves' 'spinning jenny' (Spinning)

As the flying shuttle became more widely adopted, spinners were under greater pressure to produce more yarn (thread) to keep up with the faster weaving process. The traditional spinning wheel, which produced a single thread, could not satisfy the increasing demands of the weavers, especially as demand for cloth was growing. The jenny was the first successful attempt to increase the productivity of the spinner. It initially allowed the spinner to produce eight threads simultaneously. Although it could only be used for the spinning of weft (the horizontal thread), because the thread produced was not particularly strong, the jenny was rapidly adopted in the cotton-textile industry of Hargreaves' native Lancashire. Further technological improvements to the early design soon allowed the jenny to produce up to 100 threads. Like the flying shuttle, as it was powered by hand, the jenny could be used in domestic production. Hargreaves too experienced opposition from workers fearful of a loss of employment. His home near Blackburn was destroyed in 1768.

Nevertheless, almost 20,000 jennies were in use across Lancashire by the 1780s.

1769, Richard Akwright's 'water frame' (Spinning)

Arkwright, the so-called 'father of the factory system', made two significant contributions to the technological advance of the cotton-textile industry. Firstly, the water frame was able to produce a stronger thread than the jenny, which was suitable for use as the warp (vertical thread). Although the thread produced was rather coarse in quality, by producing thread for warp and weft, the water frame enabled Lancashire manufacturers, for the first time, to produce a cloth made entirely from cotton. Secondly, the water frame, being larger than the jenny was less suited to domestic production. Arkwright recognised the potential value of factory-based production using water power. In 1771, in partnership with Jedidiah Strutt, Arkwright opened the first cotton-spinning factory in Cromford, Derbyshire. As a Lancastrian, he soon extended his factory interests across that county. So successful was the shift to factory production that, by the mid 1780s, steam engines began to be applied to the spinning factories of Lancashire, taking the technological advance of the industry a crucial step further. The use of steam freed the industry from the ties of waterside location, essential to the watermill. Access to coal became increasingly important as the steam engine rapidly demonstrated its advantages over water power.

1779, Samuel Crompton's 'mule' (Spinning)

The mule, so called because it was a cross between two machines, incorporating the better features of the jenny and the water frame, was to become the bedrock of the Lancashire spinning industry throughout the nineteenth century. The mule combined the fine quality of the thread produced by the jenny with the strength of water-frame thread. This allowed the production of a broad range of types and quality of cloth. Perhaps fortunately for the industry, Crompton did not patent his invention. His lack of business acumen allowed other manufacturers to first copy and then improve upon his design. By the early nineteenth century, spinning-machine manufacturers had developed a mule made of metal rather than wood and capable of producing up to 300 threads. In 1825, Richard Roberts' 'self acting mule' was introduced, which could spin 2,000 threads.

The impact then of spinning technologies was momentous. James Ogden, Manchester resident, in his *Description of Manchester* of 1783 recorded even then that 'large exports for foreign trade and the interior business of the country is such that no exertion by workmen could have answered the demands without the introduction of spinning machines. … It is amazing to see what thousands of spindles may be put into motion by a water wheel!'[2]

1785, Edmund Cartwright's 'power-loom' (Weaving)
The vastly increased productivity and output of cotton spinners soon created a need for similar improvements in weaving. The great increase in yarn produced was initially met with a corresponding growth of an army of handloom weavers, who, from the late eighteenth century, enjoyed a golden age which was to last until the 1830s, when power-driven, factory-based weaving finally superseded their traditional craft. What is perhaps so surprising is the length of time it took to convert weaving to a factory-based occupation. The first steps towards power looms had been made as early as 1785 when Edmund Cartwright first applied an alternative power source to the loom.

There are three principal reasons for the relatively slow adoption of factory weaving. Firstly, the power loom met with far stronger opposition than spinning had, as handloom weavers were intent upon protecting the relatively high wages they enjoyed. There were many instances of violence against factory owners who installed the new technology and against the looms themselves. The first major incident occurred in 1791, when protestors destroyed a Manchester weaving mill. The violence peaked in 1812, with 11 protestors being killed by the authorities during an attack on a factory in Middleton, near Manchester. Twelve more were hanged for their part in the protest. Secondly, the technological difficulties encountered in applying water or steam power to weaving proved more difficult to overcome than for spinning. Cartwright's loom was not without faults and a reliable and durable power loom took some time to materialise. Unlike Crompton, Cartwright had patented his machine and so it was less easy for others to improve upon without transgressing that patent. Finally, the sheer number of skilled hand-loom weavers had reduced the urgency to base weaving in factories. It was only when the power loom had been perfected, by the 1820s, that the cost advantages of factory weaving clearly outweighed those of handloom weaving. From this point, the decline of the handloom weavers began, resulting in weaving facing immense hardship in the 1840s.

The importance to industrialisation of textile technology has long been recognised. Even to contemporaries, the link between cotton textiles and steam engines was apparent. As Engels observed in 1844, 'These inventions gave rise ... to an industrial revolution which altered the whole of civil society; one, the historical importance of which is only now beginning to be recognised.'[3]

ii) Application of power to machines
Central therefore to the revolution in cotton textiles was the application of power to machinery. The role of water power especially in the

industrial revolution is often underestimated, as the more dramatic image of the steam engine has provided an enduring image of industrialisation. Yet until the 1820s, more cotton yarn was produced through the use of water power than steam. Nevertheless, the application of steam power to industrial production does mark a significant break with the past.

The steam engine had, in fact, been in use in British tin and coal mines since the start of the eighteenth century. Its use was restricted to pumping water from the mines and it was not until the last third of the century that the partnership of Matthew Boulton and James Watt modified this technology in a way which ultimately transformed manufacturing. There were two critical developments. Firstly, in 1769 James Watt had patented an improved steam engine which significantly reduced the amount of fuel needed to power the engine. Following a false start with his first business partner, John Roebuck, Watt went into partnership in 1774 with a hardware factory owner from Birmingham, Matthew Boulton. The partnership produced an engine which was cheaper to run, more reliable and technically more advanced than its predecessor. A later modification to the engine, called rotary motion, allowed steam power to drive machinery. This marked the beginning of the relationship between steam power and manufacturing and transport which lay at the heart of British industry throughout the nineteenth century. As other firms began to manufacture steam engines, so the capacity of British industry to generate steam power (and break away from the reliance upon water supplies) gained momentum.

iii) Coal reserves

The availability of huge coal reserves in Britain is central to the progress of industry. As a Swiss industrialist, Hans Escher, noted during a fact-finding visit to Britain in 1814, 'England owes its prosperity very largely to its coal deposits. Without its coal England would not have one thousandth of the factories that she now possesses.'[4] Yet technological improvement in the coal industry was limited, though some developments contributed to growing output. Better steam engines allowed deeper mines to be sunk, as flood water could be more efficiently pumped. Safety standards also improved after the Davy lamp (named after its inventor Sir Humphrey Davy) reduced, though never removed, the threat of explosion following its introduction in 1815. In the iron industry, however, technological advance was more significant.

The widespread adoption of coke as the fuel used in the smelting of iron was a watershed in the history of industrialisation. The technological breakthrough occurred in the early eighteenth century when the Darby family first successfully developed the technique. The widespread use of charcoal dominated iron production until the last third of the century as iron masters were reluctant to move to coke as it offered no clear financial advantage to do so. This changed when the cost of charcoal rose steadily after 1750. Huge coal reserves in Britain, compared to declining reserves of timber for charcoal, ensured that a potential fuel shortage did not materialise. Increasing demand for iron and the more widespread adoption of coke-fired furnaces resulted in the supply of pig iron increasing dramatically from 62,000 tons in 1780 to 340,000 tons in 1815. (Pig iron came straight from the furnace, containing some impurities.) Wrought iron (which could be worked into the required shape after reheating pig iron and then hammering out the impurities) remained costly to produce.

A second major technological advance occurred in 1784 when Henry Cort devised the 'puddling and rolling' method whereby pig iron could be heated by coal without the two materials coming into direct contact, thus ensuring that the sulphur in the coal did not contaminate the molten iron. Stirring (or puddling) the molten iron removed the carbon it contained. Rolling the now wrought iron further improved its quality and allowed the iron to be worked into the required shape, as rails, pipes or sheets. These two techniques enabled much more wrought iron to be produced at lower cost. This had the effect of boosting demand for basic pig iron and reducing Britain's imports of Swedish wrought iron. Charcoal was no longer required in any part of the iron production process and location of the industry swiftly moved to the coalfields, especially in central Scotland, South Yorkshire, the Midlands and South Wales. Further technological advances, such as Neilson's hot blast process in 1828, reduced the amount of coal used to smelt iron. This introduced hot air into the furnace (whereas bellows had previously pumped in cold air), thus maintaining a higher temperature in the furnace and reducing the amount of coal needed to fuel the furnace. Low-cost, high-quality iron was available to a range of industries including engineering, construction, machine making and later, railways and shipbuilding. In this way the iron industry epitomised the technological achievement of the industrial revolution.

iv) Innovation and the entrepreneur
The steady evolution of new techniques is only half of the story. Inventions cannot succeed without the innovatory entrepreneurial spirit which developed the potential of technological breakthrough. Although some inventors, such as Arkwright, successfully combined the roles of inventor and innovator, the greatest names of British industrialisation also included men who were able to grasp the potential of technological advance. Matthew Boulton (steam engineering), Jedidiah Strutt (cotton textiles), Josiah Wedgwood (pottery) and the Duke of Bridgewater (canals) are but some of the most famous examples of entrepreneurial achievement. Those referred to as entrepreneurs also included merchants, bankers and ship owners as well as manufacturers. Much has been made of the religious background of

the business classes. Many of these men were Nonconformists and therefore barred from holding high office such as a parliamentary seat or from taking up a university place. It has been suggested that they were therefore forced to apply their talents in other areas. Business offered such men an alternative means of achieving wealth, influence and personal ambition. Yet they were not necessarily committed to the Protestant work ethic. In any case, their business acumen may not have been as flawless as some popular images have suggested. Neither should we automatically assume these men were all formally educated or from a business background. As one observer claimed in 1833, 'Master cotton spinners and weavers, at the commencement of this important epoch, were in many instances men sprung from the ranks of the labourers ... uneducated ... of coarse habits ... but yet industrious men.'[5] Nevertheless, irrespective of their background, the favourable economic climate rewarded those with capital and confidence. High levels of demand ensured a successful period for the British entrepreneur, to the point where commercial errors were obscured by an almost guaranteed return on investment in some sectors. Nevertheless, their role remained central to industrialisation.

c) Overseas Trade

Overseas trade was an important stimulus to manufacturing and commerce. Quite apart from the provision of cheap raw materials from abroad (so vital to the expansion of cotton textiles amongst others) and overseas markets for finished products, a range of benefits accrued from overseas trade. The transport sector, most notably ports and the British merchant fleet, was a prime beneficiary. The financial sector too benefited, as the system of providing credit became more sophisticated as the complexities of international payments for goods and services required improved credit and insurance facilities. Ultimately, the financial systems which were developed to facilitate overseas trade became used also in the domestic financial sphere. This helped the longer-term development of the British financial sector and London as the world's financial capital. It should be remembered, however, that, as Macpherson noted in *Annals of Commerce* in 1805, 'The home trade is with good reason believed to be a vast deal greater in value than the whole of the foreign trade, the people of Great Britain being the best customers to the manufacturers and traders of Great Britain.'[6]

d) Financing the Industrial Revolution

Individual enterprises could be set up relatively cheaply. The small scale of early textile factories, for example, allowed many entrepreneurs to set up a cotton spinning mill by renting buildings originally used for another purpose such as a corn mill. The machinery of the early industrial revolution was also inexpensive. A weaving shed with 50 power looms could cost less than £5,000 as late as the 1830s. Nevertheless this required an initial investment of funds which not only provided buildings and technology but also sufficient monies to purchase raw materials and see the business through the early stages of operation until the first finished products were sold.

First and foremost, it is clear that more money became available to invest. On a national level, it is estimated that the proportion of Gross Domestic Product (i.e. the total value of all economic production and activity) given over to investment rose from around 6 per cent in the 1760s to over 11 per cent by the 1820s. The three key areas of investment were in industry, transport and agriculture. Figures suggest that the economy was growing generally, providing investment funds on a greater scale than ever before. Where did funding come from? Principally, capital available for investment lay in profits from existing enterprises. Agricultural profit (mainly from landlords benefiting from high rents for their land) and increasing profit from overseas trade, were fertile sources of funding. In the early stages of the industrial revolution, loans raised locally were commonly arranged through lawyers between lenders and borrowers. An equally common source of finance was borrowing from relatives or personal contacts. It is clear that borrowing from banks remained relatively unusual. Banks, particularly of the types known as the country banks, were small, often one-branch affairs. Their size made them vulnerable to short-term crises such as a sudden rush of withdrawals by local clients. This made long-term investments in industry unattractive, with the banks preferring short-term lending. It was not until the later nineteenth century that the banks came to play a more prominent role.

Loans from family, friends or local capital markets were usually obtainable at a low rate of interest. Typically, borrowing carried an annual rate of interest of 5 per cent or less, an affordable rate given the potential profit to be made in a healthy economic climate. Once an enterprise had become profitable, the most frequent source of further investment for expanding the firm was through its own profit. This source of investment, referred to as 'ploughed-back' profit, remained for many firms the staple source of funding well into the late nineteenth century. The typical private company, owned by individuals or partnerships, could satisfy its investment needs this way. As we shall see in the next section, funding for larger-scale enterprises such as canal construction required a rather different form of investment.

e) Canals and the Economy

The great rivers of Britain, including the Thames, Severn, Clyde, Humber and Trent, had long served as major transport highways.

Between the 1760s and 1830s this waterway network was comprehensively developed with the construction of 4,000 miles of canals. The outcome of this process was the linking of the emerging centres of population and industry, especially the coalfields, to the major ports, including London and many important agricultural districts.

The construction of the ten-mile Bridgewater Canal, opened in 1761 between central Manchester and the Duke of Bridgewater's coal mines at Worsley, is seen as the beginning of the 'canal age'. Its immediate success in halving coal prices in Manchester demonstrated the economic opportunities canals presented to both owners and users. Two periods of intensive investment in canals followed, firstly in the early 1770s and more specifically in 1791-99 in the period known as 'canal mania'.

Although there was no national plan for the development of the canals, by 1820 a national network existed in England. The major 'trunk' routes of the canal system are shown on the map on page 27.

The history of the canal network was inextricably linked to that of one product - coal. The principal motivation behind the construction of most canals was to improve local access to this commodity. Industrial and domestic consumers gained through the lower cost of coal as one canal barge could carry up to 50 tons, replacing expensive pack-horse transport. Mine owners benefited from the subsequent increase in demand as market prices fell. Canal companies benefited by charging tolls for the use of the canal by coal barges. The only losers appeared to be the pack horse or carriage trade, just as the handloom weavers had begun to suffer from the shift to factory-based weaving. In reducing transport costs to industry, the major consumers of coal, especially the iron industry, benefited most of all. Canals also helped improve access to wider markets for manufactured and agricultural products. The links to major ports also facilitated exports of finished products and imports of raw materials. This was especially important for the Lancashire cotton industry, as canal links to Liverpool boosted supplies and cut the cost of raw cotton. Firms might also enjoy greater flexibility when deciding where to locate. In most industrial centres canal-side location proved advantageous.

In total, £20 million was invested in the construction of Britain's canals, peaking at over £1 million per annum in the 1790s' 'canal mania'; investment which required access to substantial capital. Indeed so expensive were canals to build that the only feasible way such amounts could be raised was through the issue of shares. Landowners, merchants and manufacturers were the principal investors in canals having both the capital to invest and being, potentially, the main beneficiaries of the canal trade. For most canal projects, local capital provided the necessary funds, but for the great trunk routes, investment might come from further afield as wealthier investors recognised their potential. In the case of the busiest routes between major towns or in the major industrial centres canal

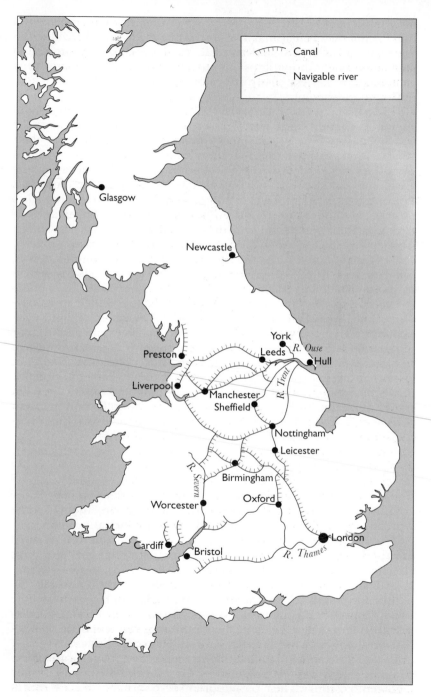

Principal inland waterways by 1830

investment could realise significant profit. Canal companies charged tolls for the use of the canal and profits from tolls were distributed in the form of dividends paid annually to shareholders. Some canals paid handsomely, though this was not always the case and many canal companies in the less busy districts of the south rarely if ever paid a return on investment.

The main benefits of canals were therefore related to the general encouragement of trade, the supply of fuel and food due to reduced transport costs. The social impact should not be ignored, as their construction provided work for tens of thousands of labourers, inland navigators or 'navvies' as they became known. At a time when the workforce was growing in number the canals were an important source of employment for many men, especially those escaping rural poverty as employment opportunities in agriculture failed to keep pace with rural population growth. For thousands of poverty-stricken Irish emigrants, and after 1815, thousands of demobilised soldiers, canal construction offered the promise of work. In economic terms, the knock-on effect of thousands of wage packets clearly had a beneficial effect on demand generally.

There were drawbacks. Some companies exploited their monopoly of local transport by charging higher tolls than was sometimes justified. The system too was complicated since canals often had different widths, and even depths, making long-distance carriage of products in one barge sometimes impossible. Also they occasionally froze in winter. Nevertheless, for all these problems the overall impact of the canals on economic and industrial growth was very significant from the 1770s onwards, not least in the provision of bulky raw materials such as coal. Even when the railways arrived, the main arterial routes remained a vital means of transport for many years.

f) The State, War and Economic Growth

The full impact of governments on the economic development of the country in this period is not yet fully understood, though some general observations can be offered. The traditional account of a State which, during the industrial revolution, steadfastly pursued *laissez-faire* economic policies, thereby creating a non-interventionist climate in which private enterprise could flourish, is, to some extent, flawed. In reality the impact of the State on the economy and the people was increasing and *laissez-faire* economic policy only became reality from the mid nineteenth century. In some respects the government's role was positive, actually contributing to economic growth. Yet, in other ways it may actually have stifled economic activity.

Today, government and its departments are major consumers of a wide range of goods and services. This was also the case in the late eighteenth century. The most important responsibility of government was the maintenance of the security of the nation. This involved maintaining order domestically and also securing the State from external threat. Yet the industrial revolution period saw Britain involved in major military conflict with the French during the Napoleonic wars of 1793-1815 and it was during wartime that the government's influence was greatest. In a negative sense, war with Napoleon resulted in a decline in consumption levels by the population as government increased general taxation to raise finance to fund the war. The introduction of income tax in 1799 affected the lower middle class upwards for the duration of the war. A purchase tax was also introduced, levied on everyday necessities such as soap, salt, and candles and therefore affecting all social classes. Luxury goods including wines, spirits and tobacco were also taxed. The consumption levels of the population were also affected by inflation, caused by the war, resulting from high government spending, shortages and increased taxation. Finally, as government spent heavily to pay for the war, so the national debt grew from £240 million in 1793 to £876 million at the end. In the longer term this ensured that after the war the government continued to raise money from various forms of taxation, especially import duties, in order to service that debt.

This negative scenario, however, should not detract too much from the economic stimulus provided by the war. War on such a scale created substantial demand for military supplies. The metal trade for weapons, woollen textiles for uniforms, food supplies for British troops and thousands of horses, leather goods, naval supplies and a host of other sectors were stimulated by the demands of war, boosting employment and output. Technical advance also quickened, stimulated by the needs of war, especially in the metal trades as the need to produce large qualities of cheaper, high-quality iron (wrought iron in particular) resulted in the widespread adoption of Cort's puddling and rolling process. Another, and perhaps unexpected, beneficiary of war was the financial sector, as government borrowing and the lending of £57 million to her allies created more efficient financial institutions experienced in dealing in government bonds. Increasing financial activity played a part in the creation of the London Stock Exchange in 1802 and the growth of banks both in London and across the country.

Thus the State played both a short-term and long-term role in economic development through its involvement in war. As Britain emerged from the war as a great military power, so her influence in the international arena increased especially at the expense of France, which suffered a serious commercial setback as a result of her defeat. The Royal Navy became the principal manifestation of British power and its subsequent role in the development of a huge empire in the post-war years is undeniable. In supporting and promoting the growth of empire, the State further encouraged economic expansion through international trade, continuing a process which had effectively begun in the previous century. To industry, the negative effects of import duties were in part offset by the security provided on major trade routes by the Royal Navy.

g) Leading Sectors

If, as the previous section suggests, a climate existed in which enterprise could flourish, what emerged were industries which exploited the new conditions. The opportunity for rapid growth was taken by a small proportion of industrial sectors which achieved levels of growth which were untypical of the economy generally. It is the achievements of these industries which effectively gave rise to claims of an industrial revolution. The success of cotton textiles, iron and coal has suggested the existence of leading sector industries and their role is seen as providing the example for others to follow. The Lancashire cotton-textile industry has provided the classic image of a leading sector industry, not only experiencing huge growth but also displacing the long-established woollen industry as the predominant manufacturing industry of the nation. The sheer scale of its achievement in terms of growth of output and employment, the shift towards factory-based production and the widespread adoption of new technologies created the image of 'King Cotton'. It is this image that we have for so long allowed to dominate our perception of the industrial revolution.

The question why cotton and not wool experienced this transformation is complex. The answer perhaps lies in the resilience of old methods of organisation and production in wool as much as in the success of the entrepreneurial spirit in cotton. The domestic system in wool remained tightly structured around the clothier because it was still in fact highly profitable and output continued to grow, albeit more slowly than cotton. The resulting conservatism of both clothier and domestic worker is therefore understandable. As a relatively new industrial sector, cotton textiles were free of the long-established traditions and vested interests which stifled technological advance of the woollen industry. The cotton sector was not regulated by guilds, unlike the woollen-textile industry. Such guilds exercised considerable power, restricting access to the trade and protecting the vested interests of clothiers. In Lancashire, the absence of guilds assisted the growth of the industry, as James Ogden noted in 1783: 'Nothing has more contributed to the improvements in trade here than the free admission of workmen … whereby the trade has been kept open to strangers of every description who contribute to its improvement by their ingenuity.'[7] Cotton masters proved to be more receptive to new technology, and in spinning in particular. This allowed a relatively rapid shift towards factory-based production in the last quarter of the eighteenth century. A clear division of labour therefore developed in the cotton-textile sector, with specialist spinning and weaving sectors, and even the development of specialist spinning and weaving towns.

Lancashire, and to a lesser extent Derbyshire, Lanarkshire, became the British cotton-textile centres. Lancashire came to dominate, possessing a range of adva▚▚▚▚ ▚▚hich encouraged the rapid expansion of the cotton trade ▚▚▚▚▚▚ Lancashire and the West Indies and the southern states ▚▚▚SA. Improved canal links between Liverpool and the Manchester area improved the industry's access to raw materials and reduced its transport costs. The Pennine hills provided a reliable supply of water, used in the provision of water power and finishing processes, and the Lancashire coalfield provided the essential fuel as steam power emerged. Furthermore, the existence of a tradition of textile production, including linen and wool, had provided a workforce with the necessary skills. As demand for cotton textiles increased, helped by the removal of duties on cotton cloth in 1774, so Lancashire's expertise developed. Technology, cheaper transport, specialist factory production and the cut in duty all combined to reduce the cost in real terms of cotton cloth by two thirds between 1780 and 1812. This further boosted demand, and the industry experienced spiralling growth rates in production far in excess of woollen textiles, averaging 12 per cent per annum between 1780 and 1790, compared to an average growth rate for the industrial sector generally of 2.8 per cent. In 1800 cotton cloth accounted for a quarter of all exports by volume, compared with just 2 per cent in 1780. Cotton textiles thus became a driving force of the British industrial revolution, though the very fact that it was so exceptional should sound a note of caution. Changes across the economy as a whole do not live up to claims of an industrial revolution so easily.

4 An Agricultural Revolution?

Growing levels of output and productivity were not restricted to industry. Other sectors, including transport and the financial sector, were also affected. Agriculture too benefited from and contributed to the growth in economic activity.

Some historians have even referred to an 'agricultural revolution'. The same debates relating to the nature, timing and extent of change already discussed for industry apply to agriculture, and broadly similar conclusions have been reached. Once again, whether or not those changes are deserving of the description 'revolution' is a question which is largely redundant. The important thing is that we understand what happened, not how we label it.

a) The Nature of Change

A quickening in the pace of enclosure is generally held to be a major aspect of the modernisation of British agriculture from the second half of the eighteenth century. In the century after 1750 over 4,000 separate acts of Parliament resulted in the enclosure of 20 per cent (2.4 million hectares) of the cultivated land, effectively completing the enclosure of the land. A second aspect of change was the extension of the amount of land being cultivated, especially in the arable sector. The sown area rose from 10 million acres in 1750 to 15 million by 1850, most of which was given over to grain crops such as wheat, barley and oats. Finally, the increased adoption of more modern techniques affected both pastoral and arable sectors, especially that of improved crop rotation.

Traditionally, in the open-field system, two years of cultivation were followed by one year when the land was left fallow. This allowed an opportunity for the soil to recover. The new system, often referred to as four-course rotation, had first been used in Britain in the early eighteenth century. Its later more widespread adoption in arable and mixed-farming areas did much to improve the soil, boost crop yields and support a larger livestock population. Year one in this rotation saw the cultivation of wheat, followed by a year where the field was given over to clover. This served a dual purpose as clover put nitrogen, an essential nutrient, back into the soil. Cattle or sheep grazed on the clover, providing natural animal fertiliser to further enrich the soil. A further cereal crop such as barley or oats was followed in year four by turnip production. This final crop also provided nutrients and had the further advantage of providing winter feed for livestock. Thus more animals avoided winter slaughter and the body weight of livestock was boosted, increasing meat production. The growth of mixed farming and an improvement in arable and pastoral yields became a feature of the latter half of the eighteenth century.

b) Explaining Agricultural Change

There is no doubt however that the most important motivation behind agricultural improvement was the opportunity to boost profits. Landowners recognised that encouraging enclosure would ultimately allow the application of new techniques. The new methods, boosting the fertility of the soil and yields, would in turn allow them to set higher rents as farms became more profitable. This was further encouraged by a steadily rising demand for agricultural products as the growth in population stimulated food production. Furthermore, the Napoleonic wars and the inflation they created boosted the price of agricultural products. High prices encouraged increased production, and many farmers were persuaded to increase the amount of land they cultivated, although there were examples of farmers bringing land into cultivation which did not always produce high yields. These marginal lands were quickly abandoned when prices fell after the Napoleonic wars (see the bar chart over leaf).

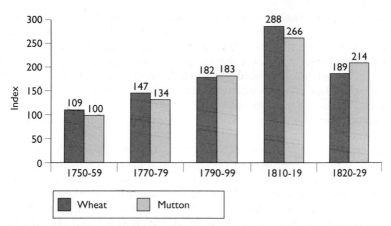

Index of average annual prices per decade of wheat and mutton, 1750-1829

If profit provided the motive then agricultural publicists provided the information. A number of significant individuals have been singled out as providing the role models for British farmers, and influential publications ensured that knowledge was disseminated across the agricultural sector.

The work of Robert Bakewell in improved livestock breeding, Viscount Townshend for developing four-course rotation and Jethro Tull in inventing the seed drill are often cited as examples of agricultural innovators of the mid eighteenth century whose work influenced later generations. In reality more emphasis should be placed on the spread of knowledge and the profit motive in persuading farmers to adopt new approaches. Thomas Coke, Arthur Young and William Marshall, amongst others, were closely involved in providing the means by which ideas could spread. Arthur Young's *A six week tour through the Southern counties* (1768) and the periodical *Annals of Agriculture*, together with William Marshall's *A General Survey of the Rural Economy of England* (1787), provided useful surveys of the nature of agricultural practice. We know that such works enabled farmers to receive information regarding practices such as crop rotation, drainage, marling (the use of marl, a form of clay, to improve sandy soils) and hoeing. The agricultural show was another forum through which ideas could reach many farmers. The government too recognised the benefits of a more dynamic agricultural sector, creating the Board of Agriculture in 1793.

c) The Economic Impact of Agricultural Improvement

So how important was agriculture to the process of industrialisation? Essentially, its role was fourfold. Even the most pessimistic view of agricultural change recognises that in overall terms there was a significant increase in total production and of average yield per acre in the latter half of the eighteenth century. The essential outcome of this was that the rapidly growing urban population remained fed. The extent to which agriculture served the domestic market is demonstrated by the fact that by the 1780s Britain was no longer a net exporter of wheat. The home market consumed all that British agriculture could produce, with high demand ensuring high prices. The absence of long-term food shortages helped ensure that society remained relatively stable, assisting the creation of a climate in which the economy grew. Agricultural labourers and their families may have experienced high levels of poverty, but even so the employment of over a million agricultural workers ensured that rural society was an important source of demand. Landowners (who already included many of the wealthiest families in Britain) and more prosperous farmers were given a significant boost by high prices and high levels of demand. This ensured also that profits from agriculture provided a significant source of investment, especially in canal building and local industrial initiatives.

Agriculture was not only concerned with the supply of food. It is often forgotten that a wide range of industrial raw materials originated in the agricultural sector, including grains for distilling and animal products for the woollen textiles, leather, candle and soap industries. Thus rural England was both supplier of, and customer to, the manufacturing sector and remained a key sector of the economy.

5 Conclusion

For over half a century, then, the country had witnessed an upturn in the process of industrialisation, and in doing so established Britain in the eyes of the world as a potent economic force. Still, there are many things we do not fully understand regarding this experience.

Firstly, although we have identified a wide range of factors that encouraged economic growth, we cannot state with any certainty the relative importance of any one factor against another. It is important to recognise that no single 'cause' stands in isolation and that any attempt to explain the industrial revolution must consider the very complex series of inter-linking relationships between the factors identified. Let us consider one such 'cause' of accelerated growth, for example the growth of the canal network. This may have stimulated demand as it reduced prices for some commodities such as coal, by cutting transport costs. However, without other factors such as the growing availability of capital to invest in canals, or of the growing population demanding more coal or the growth of industries that needed improved transport, the canal network would not have developed as it did. Thus the growing canal network was both a cause and consequence of the industrial revolution.

Secondly, we must also ask if the absence of one or more of the causes identified would have restricted industry to the point where economic growth could not have taken off as it did. The experiences of Britain's European competitors might suggest that this was the case. France, for example, possessed many of the possible pre-requisites for economic growth, including raw materials in abundance, population growth, overseas colonial possessions and a traditional manufacturing sector. Yet she did not enjoy the relative political stability of Britain, and it has been suggested that political uncertainty, amongst other factors, may have restricted French economic growth. Similarly, the Dutch, with a sophisticated financial sector, more productive agriculture and strong overseas trade links, failed to emulate British growth.

Thirdly, we must ensure that we keep a sense of perspective when assessing the changes that occurred in the economy. In particular, reservations exist with regard to the actual achievements of both industry and agriculture.

a) Reservations about Industry

i)   Frequently economic historians have presented economic growth in terms of aggregate figures, reflecting the fortunes of the national economy. This 'macro-economic' approach can present a distorted picture of what was actually happening at a more specific or 'micro-economic' level. There was in fact little uniformity between the varied sectors of the economy. For example, we have seen that cotton textiles were growing at a much faster rate than most other industries. In other words, it is worth remembering that averages are constructed from data that contain two extremes. In the case of the British economy, a two-tier industrial sector was emerging with cotton, iron and coal in particular occupying a position of elevated importance, with the more typical experience being of slower rates of growth across industry generally.

ii) Care must also be taken not to exaggerate the technological aspect of economic growth. In more typical sectors of the economy, the factory, that cherished manifestation of industrial revolution, remained stubbornly absent. Most people did not work in factories. The census of 1841 tells us that a maximum of 12 per cent of the employed workforce were employed in factories. Even in cotton textiles, in the weaving sector, there were three handloom weavers for every factory weaver in the 1830s. In other words, traditional skills and practices survived the industrial revolution. As the 1851 census showed, over half of employers who filled in returns employed fewer than five people. Typically, low levels of productivity remained and, for most workers, steam power played no part in their working lives.

Where technological advance had taken place, it was frequently the result of trial and error, adapting existing practice rather than the creation of radical new ideas whose origins lay in scientific research. Indeed there is very little evidence of any widespread or systematic appliance of science to industry until the mid-nineteenth century.

iii) The regional nature of the industrial revolution might prompt us to question the whole idea of a 'British' industrial revolution. As we have noted, specific areas of the country developed expertise in a range of industrial regions. It is equally true that, for many parts of the kingdom, little or no evidence existed of an industrial revolution. The following table, derived from the 1841 census, which gives us the first reliable employment statistics, indicates the range of regional variation for male employment between industrial and non-industrial areas.

Occupational Variations for Selected Counties (% of total) and Occupational Sectors, 1841

	Manufacturing	Mining	Agriculture
Buckinghamshire	20	0	52
Bedfordshire	20	0	55
Cambridgeshire	19	0	53
Scottish Highlands	15	0	62
Lancashire	35	4	10
Durham	31	20	14
Strathclyde	42	6	18
Yorkshire, West Riding	54	5	14

b) Agriculture and Economic Growth

Any assessment of the role of agriculture in the economy is also contentious. High levels of production and strong profits for landowners and efficient farmers can easily disguise areas of weakness. It must be remembered that:

i)   Increases in production failed to keep pace with total population growth, so that Britain became dependent upon imported foodstuffs, especially from Ireland. An annual average surplus of wheat of 1.3 million quarters per annum in 1760-69 had become a deficit of 1.2 million by 1800.

ii)   Many of the changes which exemplify the progress of the period had in fact been known of for many decades. Slow, steady change, moving from a desperately inefficient open-field system is perhaps a more appropriate description than revolution. Indeed the very low productivity of the open-field system serves only to exaggerate the improvements in yields and productivity achieved after enclosure.

iii) The ability of British agriculture to boost production owed most to the fact that more land was coming under the plough. Most farmers therefore increased production in times of high prices simply by increasing acreages cultivated. Many farmers, particularly those working the smaller farms of around 50 acres or less, could not afford to change their practices. In the more remote areas poor dissemination of knowledge and inherent conservatism ensured the survival of traditional methods.

iv) The high price paid for foodstuffs, particularly in the Napoleonic wars, suggests that (unlike the cotton-textile industries, where productivity improvements resulted in falling prices) agricultural practices still required considerable improvement.

v) The decline of prices after the Napoleonic wars resulted in agricultural depression, thus indicating the fragile base of the so-called 'agricultural revolution'.

vi) There was a great deal of severe poverty in rural areas as the agricultural labouring classes were victims of high food prices. Thousands sought alternative employment in industrial areas or in canal construction, or depended upon the Poor Law. For a sector of rural society, enclosure could harm cultivators of small landholdings. As they were unable to contribute to the cost of enclosing the land, many were forced to sell, becoming 'day labourers' on the new farms. Arthur Young observed that 'There is, however, one class of farmers which has greatly suffered by enclosures; these are the little farmers … it is an evil to them, which is to be regretted.'[8]

vii) The application and use of technology has often been seriously overstated. The main technological advance was in the production of better-quality iron ploughs rather than the adoption of agricultural machinery.

Recent studies of agricultural change, then, have sought to downplay its role as a stimulus to economic and industrial growth. It was a vital player in a supporting role, but claims of an agricultural revolution which played a central role in the industrial revolution are exaggerated, as the relative positions of industry and agriculture in the economy were progressively reversed.

In conclusion, the industrial revolution was a process of change which represented a speeding up of an evolutionary change whose origins lay further back than 1780. Growth was not a new phenomenon, but the accelerated pace of growth became more noticeable for the last quarter of the eighteenth century. For most of that century, developments in transport, agriculture, population levels, new technologies, overseas trade and the financial sectors began to materially affect the way the country's industries operated. Traditional forms of production co-existed with new processes for many decades to come, but, crucially, the transformation had begun: the age of the machine had arrived.

References
1   Alasdair Clayre (ed), *Nature and Industrialisation* (Open University Press, 1977), p. 1.
2   Peter Lane, *Documents on British Economic and Social History 1750-1870* (Macmillan, 1978), p. 20.
3   Friedrich Engels, *The Condition of the Working Class in England* (Granada, 1982), p. 37.
4   Trevor May, *The Economy 1815-1914* (Collins, 1980), p. 8.
5   E. Royston Pike, *Human Documents of the Industrial Revolution in Britain* (Allen & Unwin, 1966), p. 46.
6   Richard Brown, *Economic Revolution in Britain 1750-1850* (Cambridge University Press, 1992), p. 91.
7   Lane, *Documents on British Economic and Social History 1750-1870*, p. 20.
8   Mark Overton, *Agricultural Revolution in England* (Cambridge University Press, 1996), p. 177.

Answering essay questions on 'The Industrial Revolution'

The industrial revolution has proved to be a fertile area for examination questions. Indeed the ingenuity and inventiveness of examiners in creating a wide range of demanding essay titles has tested both teacher and student for many years. Although it is only possible here to present a small sample of actual examples, we can identify types of questions, suggesting four separate categories:

1.   Those questions which deal on a general level with the whole idea of an industrial revolution. Was there an industrial revolution? What developments took place if an industrial revolution did occur? When did it occur? And of course, what factors caused the industrial revolution?
2.   Many questions deal very specifically with individual industries, especially the staple industries of cotton textiles, iron and coal, and the agricultural sector. Such questions usually require students to outline and explain developments in those industries in the late eighteenth and early nineteenth centuries. It is common for examiners to provide statistics relating to output or exports and ask students to explain the increases shown.
3.   You will need to be aware of the role of individual 'causes' of the industrial revolution, as identified in Section 3 of this chapter, assessing the importance of their contribution to economic development. Favoured topics include the entrepreneur, transport developments (especially canals), investment capital, and agriculture. Many questions will expect

you to show some knowledge of each 'cause' before and after the years of the industrial revolution. You may even be asked to compare the relative contributions of more than one 'cause'.

4. The economic and social implications of change, for example of canal construction or agricultural enclosure, is also a common type of question. As this book deals specifically with economic factors you should ensure that your further reading deals with the social history of industrialisation. Economic history and social history are inextricably linked and you should be able to demonstrate an awareness of the common ground they share.

Consider the following examples:

1. What were the principal factors which contributed to the accelerated economic growth of Britain in the period referred to as the 'industrial revolution'?
2. 'After more than thirty years of research, we are still no nearer discerning the causes of the industrial revolution.' Discuss.
3. Explain the growth of the Lancashire cotton industry during the period c. 1770-c. 1850.
4. Assess the contribution of developments in inland transport to economic expansion between 1750 and 1830.
5. What were the economic and social consequences of agricultural innovation in England between 1750 and 1830?

The above examples not only address different subjects but also call for different approaches. Question 1 is very straightforward, simply calling for an appreciation of the range of factors that, taken as a whole, boosted industrial output and economic growth. You should demonstrate an awareness of how separate factors may be linked to others in the list. Question 2 requires students not only to understand the idea of an industrial revolution but also to demonstrate an awareness of the nature of the historiographical debate. This does not call for a 'yes' or 'no' type answer. Question 3, on the other hand, requires the student to demonstrate an awareness of the specific factors which resulted in the growth of a specific industry. This may be dealt with as a list of factors, perhaps in order of importance. However, the question 'Why Lancashire?' is easily missed. Question 4 tests your ability to evaluate the importance of the development of one sector in the overall context of economic growth. This is a more demanding question than 3 and you will be required to demonstrate an awareness of the interrelationships that existed across the economy. Question 5 is broader still and a strong answer to this question will explore the positive and negative aspects of change, recognising that apparent economic progress often had negative social implications.

In attempting to answer any essay question, there are a few fundamental rules to follow. Firstly you should ensure that you are fully aware of what the question means. The greatest sin committed in essay writing is in succumbing to the temptation to write all you know about a topic. Take time to decipher the question. Once you know what is required, a useful tip is to construct an essay plan on, say, one side of A4 paper. Your introduction, actually more important than many students appreciate, should preferably be one paragraph and indicate your understanding of the question and outline the nature of the argument to come. This sets the tone for the essay and should create a favourable impression on the marker.

The second section of the essay is the longest, providing the bulk of your answer. This is where you provide the historical evidence which delivers what you promise in the introduction. Careful subdivision of this section into individual paragraphs, preferably linked, will enable you to provide a coherent answer which focuses on the relevant issues. At all times ask yourself the question, 'Is this paragraph contributing to answering the set question, i.e. is it relevant?'

Your conclusion is also important. A short paragraph in conclusion should summarise your argument without repeating the same points. It should contain your actual answer to the question set if you have not already done this in the introduction.

Follow this pattern for the essay titles provided at the end of subsequent chapters. For most students the essay-plan technique will help improve the focus and relevance of answers. Written in note form, with key headings for each paragraph, it will provide a shorthand version of an essay answer and prove to be a useful aid to revision and examination practice.

Summary Diagram
The Industrial Revolution

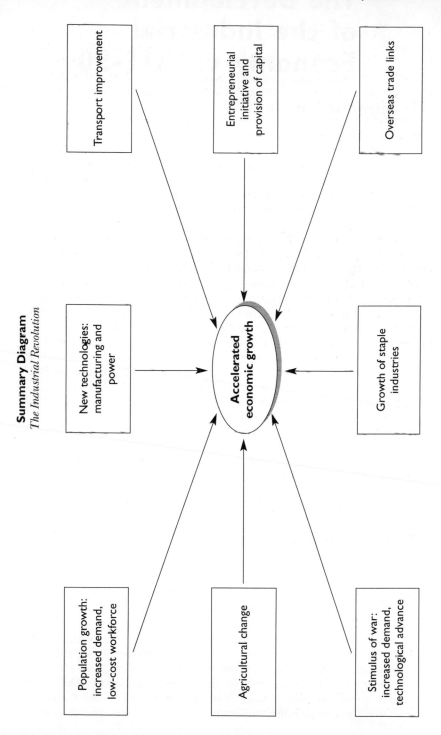

3 The Development of the Industrial Economy, c. 1815-50

1 Introduction

If the industrial revolution had provided the initial boost to the industrialisation process, then the three decades or so following the Napoleonic wars witnessed the development of a truly industrial economy. Manufacturing and mining replaced agriculture as the principal source of national wealth. Trade and transport generated almost as much wealth as the agricultural sector by 1851 (see page 10).

The transition from industrial revolution to industrial economy was not a smooth one. This was a complex time when overall economic growth was punctuated by times of usually short, though occasionally, serious recession. Nevertheless, great strides were made towards the industrialisation of the nation, generating huge wealth in the process. In this chapter we shall examine the development of the economy and the increasingly important role of the middle-class capitalist. The extension of middle-class economic and political influence is reflected in the growing importance of large-scale industrial enterprise and the victory of the free-trade lobby. Similarly, the mobilisation of huge financial resources allowing the construction of the railway network is testament to the commercial success of the nation. All of these issues are examined here.

There are, of course, two sides to the industrialisation story, and the human responses to changing economic fortune display a working class (or classes) often ill at ease with the consequences of industrial growth. Deteriorating urban conditions, social unrest, and a threat of political revolution in the 1815-50 period are reminders that economic success did not automatically pervade all ranks of society.

2 The Progress of Capitalism

There is a great deal of evidence that supports the claim that this was a period of clear economic advance. Capitalism may be said to have 'progressed' in that the main sectors associated with the developing capitalist economy (especially manufacturing, mining, trade, transport and the financial sector) all experienced very significant growth in this period. This success is manifested in the rapid growth of industrial output. The development of the staple industries of iron, coal and cotton textiles is unquestionable and iron and coal, in particular, may be viewed as barometers of the economic climate. Both these sectors provided the crucial raw materials of industrialisation. Iron was used in a huge variety of ways, from the manufacture of steam engines and textile machines, to construction and domestic implements.The railway too depended on a strong iron industry, rising to the challenge of increased demand. Production soared and prices fell as the following table indicates:

Growth of the Iron Industry, 1820-49		
Year (Annual average over 5-year period)	Pig Iron Production ('000 tons)	Total Value of Pig Iron Produced (£ million)
1820-24	428	11.0
1825-29	658	17.8
1830-34	689	13.7
1835-39	1,150	22.7
1840-44	1,278	19.0
1845-49	2,000	34.4

Over the same period, the output of coal rose from 17 to 48 million tons. Such increases were not restricted to the staple industries. Glass, brickmaking, brewing, woollen textiles, and more besides, experienced impressive levels of growth. The chief beneficiary of industrial expansion was, of course, the capitalist. Manufacturers were developing new production techniques and placing greater emphasis than ever before on efficiency and competitiveness, often becoming highly specialised in one branch of production. To the capitalist employer, it became imperative that industry should operate with minimal intervention to allow a firm to compete effectively. The case for *laissez-faire* economics was presented with greater force in this period, culminating in the campaign for free trade in the 1830s and 1840s.

For the industrial worker, the drive towards greater specialisation created a greater division of labour, whereby the worker would specialise in a particular task rather than carry out a variety of functions. This division of labour was strengthened by the more widespread adoption of machinery in place of human effort. Whilst not necessarily enhancing the work experience of the employee, this improved efficiency was a key feature of the industrial economy, allowing British manufacturers to out-compete their rivals and boast of being the 'Workshop of the World' by the mid century. The share of national income attributable to manufacturing and mining rose from 20 per cent in 1811 to 34 per cent in 1851. This was largely achieved at the expense of agriculture, which saw an almost exact reversal of its influence, declining from 35 per cent to 20 per cent over the same period.

3 Cause for Concern

Despite the overall economic expansion of the period, it is important to be aware that growing national prosperity was not the result of unqualified or uninterrupted growth. Indeed, at times, the economy experienced periods of serious downturn as unexpected and shocking to the capitalist as it was materially harmful to the worker. In the immediate aftermath of victory in the Napoleonic wars in 1815, the economy entered a period of depression as government war contracts dried up, European exports declined and over a quarter of a million demobilised troops flooded the labour market. This period of economic malaise continued until recovery began from 1821. Further, short-lived trade recessions occurred in 1826 and 1830, though the vulnerability of the economy to a slump in trade, especially the export industries, was most vividly demonstrated between 1837 and 1842. In these years, Britain experienced the most severe recession of the nineteenth century. It was blamed on a number of factors, including a fall in demand for British products overseas. At home, poor harvests had boosted food prices, reducing the income available for spending on manufactured products. Compounding the difficulties was a dip in railway construction between 1840 and 1842. The revival of trade from 1843 was briefly interrupted by another short recession during 1847 and 1848, before the economy launched into the boom years of the 1850s and 1860s.

Agriculture too showed serious signs of strain, although this sector largely failed to break out of the stagnation and recession which affected industry more sporadically. The experience of agriculture in the post-war years, if contemporary accounts provided by farmers and landowners were to be believed, was of continuing difficulties. Whether or not this constituted a depression, as many contemporaries claimed, is debatable. Certainly the post-war collapse of high war-time prices contributed to a period of stagnation which was to last until the late 1840s. The problems were most acute in the grain sector. Bumper harvests in 1814 pushed down the price of wheat as prices fell rapidly from their peak, in 1812, of 126 shillings per quarter (quarter of a ton; a common measurement for dealing in corn in the eighteenth and nineteenth centuries). By the end of the decade they had fallen to 67 shillings per quarter. Thereafter, wheat prices averaged only 56 shillings per quarter from 1820 to 1850, reaching their lowest price of just 39 shillings in 1835 and peaking at 70 shillings in the poor harvest of 1839.

As landowners still dominated Parliament, assistance from government to protect farmers from falling prices had been swift to materialise. In 1815, fearing that falling prices would continue if foreign grain was allowed into Britain, Parliament passed the Corn Laws. These laws, by prohibiting the importation of foreign wheat, until the price of the home-grown product reached 80 shillings per quarter, sought to protect farmers' incomes. This would also protect the incomes of the landowners by allowing them to maintain rents at high levels. Prices, as we have seen, did not recover to war-time levels, or even the 80 shilling mark. Improvements to the land and favourable weather conditions produced a series of good harvests, keeping prices down. In reality, for many farmers the fall in prices was offset by the improved yields and strong demand at home as population rose. However, problems occurred for those farmers and landowners who had borrowed heavily to improve their land in the years of high prices. For some farmers debt repayments could not be met as prices fell. Similarly, some landowners who had funded improvements could not afford to lower rents in line with price falls as they too needed to repay the debts which improvements had incurred. Low prices for some, therefore, created genuine difficulty. However, it must be noted that the vociferous claims of agricultural depression, largely emanating from the landed classes, were exaggerated. For the agricultural labourer, distress was genuine (see page 56). For the farmer and landowner, low prices were offset by better yields per acre, high demand, an absence of foreign competition and low-labour costs. For those involved in the rearing of animals, i.e. in the pastoral sector, prices did not fall so far as wheat, and cheaper grains meant lower feed prices. Clearly, the unique conditions of wartime had boosted prices. Peacetime brought with it a return to normal prices, and we must therefore treat claims of agricultural depression with care.

4 The Economy and the Middle Classes

Any assessment of the growth of the industrial economy must take into account the unique and crucial role of the capitalist middle classes. The manufacturer, merchant, banker and other professional classes together make up the middle classes who played such an important role in economic development. Industrialisation did not, of course, create the middle class. A thriving middle class existed in the eighteenth century and before. What happened from the industrial revolution onward, and particularly from the years after the Napoleonic wars, was a growth in the power and influence of the middle classes. Increased personal wealth and a more prominent role in the creation of the nation's wealth helped ensure that the previously unchallenged economic supremacy of the landed aristocracy came under threat. Increasingly, then, the economic policies of the nation came to reflect the preferences and priorities of the middle classes. As industry and commerce superseded agriculture as the dominant forces in the economy, so the middle classes demanded and won greater influence over government policy. In 1832, the 'Great Reform Act' enfranchised middle-class men. In 1835 the Municipal Corporations Act brought greater democracy to local government and effectively passed control of the industrial towns and cities to the middle classes. In social terms, the middle classes had extended their influence over the lives of millions with the rise of new industries and new ways of working.

Inevitably, aristocratic privilege and influence declined as a result. Even the great bastion of landed power, the Tory Party, was not immune, a fact vividly demonstrated by the accession to the leadership of Sir Robert Peel, the son of a Lancashire cotton-textile manufacturer. The landed aristocracy was not displaced as the dominant force in the Commons overnight. However, the free-trade debate, from the late 1830s onward, is a clear indication that the economic policies of the nation were in future to be determined by the demands of industry and commerce rather than the land.

a) The Free-Trade Debate

In 1776, the economist Adam Smith published *The Wealth of Nations*, which was to prove to be of immense influence in the development of the British economy in the nineteenth century. The basic premise of Smith's work was that a nation's economy, including industrial development and trading system, should be left to develop naturally, without intervention from government. Furthermore, tariffs, i.e. duties on imports, hindered the most effective development of an economy by protecting inefficient producers from competition. This worked against the interests of the consumer, keeping prices artificially high, benefiting only the interests of the producer.

A policy of non-interventionism and free trade (often referred to as *laissez-faire*) as promoted by Smith and further developed in the nineteenth century by David Ricardo and others, clearly clashed with Britain's long tradition of State intervention. This policy of intervention, or mercantilism, which had been in operation since Tudor times, consisted of a range of policies. Tariffs on imports were the central feature of this protectionism, with some products, such as Indian cotton actually banned from Britain altogether. Domestic industry benefited from a lack of competition whilst government income was boosted from the money raised from import duties. A second strand to mercantilism involved the Navigation Laws, of 1651 and 1660, which strictly controlled the trade between Britain and her colonies, ensuring that imports to Britain were carried in British vessels or those of the country of origin. Thirdly, the economic development of British colonies was controlled, in order to guarantee that the colonists provided Britain with raw materials and in return bought British manufactures. Fourthly, the British government granted sole trading rights to commercial companies (such as the East India Company in 1763) between Britain and specific regions of the world. Finally, in order to maintain Britain's advantage, the export of some machinery was prohibited to stop competitors benefiting from British technical expertise. For the same reason, some skilled craftsmen were not allowed to emigrate. From an economic point of view, the policy had seemed to be successful. Britain had displaced the Dutch as Europe's primary trading nation, while the Empire had expanded by 1815 to include Canada, Australia, and territories in southern Africa, in the West Indies, India and the Pacific. Any challenge to mercantilism therefore had major hurdles to overcome.

The case presented for free trade had, despite the apparent success of mercantilism, won some influential early converts. William Pitt the Younger, Prime Minister in 1783-1801 and 1804-06 had, for example, initiated steps to reduce tariffs between Britain and France. However, the outbreak of war with France from 1793, and thus the need to boost government revenue, postponed any move toward tariff reduction. Thus the first significant action to promote free trade came after the Napoleonic wars. The theoretical case for free trade had, by 1815, won some support in government and the civil service. The experience of a long and costly military conflict with the French had strengthened support for the free traders' assertion that the removal of tariffs reduced the likelihood of war, as nations, encouraged by free trade, developed links with each other. To those involved in the day to day realities of business, however, it was essential to make a convincing practical case for free trade. In this respect, the free-trade lobby was to win over the middle classes *en masse*.

A persuasive argument for free trade suggested that Britain, as the world's premier manufacturing and trading nation, no longer needed the protection of tariffs against overseas competition. The abolition of tariffs would boost the importation of cheap raw materials and thus lower the cost of British manufactured goods. Naturally, this would ensure greater sales, and the prospect of a boost to exports proved attractive to those industries such as cotton textiles and iron goods, for which the export trade was vital. It was no coincidence that in the serious recession of 1837-42, many more manufacturers became converts to the cause of free trade. The prominent free trader Richard Cobden argued, in 1835, that Britain's future as the world's major industrial power would be under threat should free trade not be adopted. In particular, he cited the case of trade between Britain and the United States in support of tariff removal. It was expected that, if American products were allowed into Britain tariff-free, the United States would reciprocate. Thus, as the United States provided the bulk of Britain's raw-cotton supplies, free trade with the supplier would guarantee a supply of cheap raw cotton, ensuring the competitiveness of the British cotton industry. This, furthermore, would protect the livelihoods of the cotton workers and their dependants, who numbered almost one million people. Similarly, free trade with the United States would also boost the export trades, as 25 per cent of British exports went to the United States.

Such practical arguments proved to be vital in swaying the Lancashire cotton interest, the staunchest advocates of free trade. Manchester was to become the centre of commercial support for the campaign, together with Liverpool, whose merchants, ship owners and other professionals relished the prospect of a boom in international trade and the consequent economic results. For governments, free trade would resolve the endemic problem of smuggling, which, it was claimed, illegally occupied up to 40,000 people around Britain's coastline.

The idea of free trade was sold to the lower classes on the basis of cheap food and better employment prospects. Under a free-trade system, the hated Corn Laws, which had been branded as a 'bread tax', would be repealed. Also, the anticipated boost to exports would protect existing jobs and create many more besides. To the worker, lower food prices held an obvious attraction. To the employer, lower food prices might also keep down wage rates, though few publicly voiced this as a factor influencing their support. Inevitably, the principal source of opposition to free trade came from the agricultural sector, especially the arable interests of the south and south-east, who feared that cheap foreign grain would flood the British market, further depressing already low prices.

b) Achieving Free Trade

The eventual success of the free-trade movement resulted from the ability of key individuals and the business community generally to relate the theoretical advantages of free trade to the events and economic climate of the time. The first tentative steps towards a reduction in tariffs were taken soon after the publication of *The Wealth of Nations*. The Pitt-Vergennen treaty of 1786 reduced the tariffs imposed by the British and French on each others' products. Pitt, in justifying the move, had referred to the commercial opportunities this offered, describing France as 'a market of so many millions of people - a market so near and prompt - a market of certain return'.[1] However, the advent of war deferred the issue until tariff reform emerged as a force once more in the 1820s.

The post-war recession had forced economists, businessmen and politicians alike to consider the economic performance of the nation more closely. By 1820, the Board of Trade had become dominated by disciples of Adam Smith. Most favoured a shift from protectionist policies. The Select Committee of the House of Commons on Overseas Trade, which reported in July 1820, was rigged by the free-trade lobby. It claimed that restrictions on trade 'have a tendency to cramp the operations of commerce and to impede the growth of opulence.'[2] In recommending a move toward lower tariffs, the committee set in place the grounds for tariff reform. Between 1823 and 1827, Board of Trade President, William Huskisson, and

Chancellor of the Exchequer Frederick Robinson initiated measures which reduced tariffs on imports of raw materials to 10 per cent (which, in the case of some products, had been as high as 40 per cent). There was some relaxation on the restrictions on the export of British machinery, and skilled workers were allowed to emigrate. The Navigation Laws were relaxed, allowing in more foreign ships and easing the draconian trade restrictions on the colonies. Even the Corn Laws were amended, introducing a sliding scale of duties.

The improvements in trade and business generally, together with the domination of Parliament by electoral reform issues in the following ten years, saw the free-trade debate subside until the return of recession in 1837. This time, the ideological case for free trade was supported much more powerfully by the manufacturing interest. Now the middle classes were in a stronger position, wielding greater economic and political power. They had also become more aware of the practical case for free trade and thus devoted considerable energy to achieving far more radical demands than merely tariff reduction. Free trade was demanded and the issue became a battleground between the old economic order, dominated by the landed classes, and the forces of industrial capitalism.

In the vanguard of the free-trade movement was the Anti-Corn-Law League, founded in Manchester in 1838, representing the free-trade aspirations of the industrial and commercial middle class. It was this class who had perhaps most to gain from free trade. This might occur either through the direct benefits free trade would bring to their individual firm or by the anticipated boost to the economy generally. By focussing its attention on the Corn Laws, the League aimed to destroy the very symbol of protectionism and of the selfish interest of the landed classes. Clearly, the intention was the removal of all tariffs and the advent of completely free trade, though the Corn Laws were particularly reviled, keeping bread prices artificially high and increasing pressure for higher wages. The leading figure of the League, textile manufacturer Richard Cobden, saw the campaign as more than the conflict between two conflicting economic ideas. It marked an attack on the privileged landed aristocracy, whom he described as 'the bread taxing oligarchy [a small, exclusive class], unprincipled, rapacious, unfeeling and plundering.'[3]

Cobden and his leading colleague in the League, John Bright, a Rochdale cotton manufacturer, became MPs for northern industrial constituencies in the early 1840s. This allowed the free-trade message to be put more directly to Parliament, where increasingly the campaign won over supporters. In 1841, at the height of the recession, Sir Robert Peel became the new Tory Prime Minister. The Peel family fortune had been made in the manufacture of cotton textiles and his support for tariff reduction resulted in two major free-trade budgets during his administration, in 1842 and 1845, effectively putting Britain on the road to free trade. There were major reductions in tariffs on food and raw materials, most falling to a maximum of 5 per cent. To maintain government revenue, income tax was reintroduced at 7d (almost 3p) in the pound on incomes over £150 per annum. All restrictions were removed on machine exports, boosting the engineering industry. By the end of 1845, Peel's government had removed entirely import duties on over 500 items.

The Corn Laws, however, were more problematic. The Tory party, traditionally representing the landed interests, was seriously divided over the Corn Laws. The anti-repeal faction, led by the charismatic Benjamin Disraeli, fiercely resisted repeal, fearing the ruin of British agriculture. The Whigs, on the other hand, supported repeal. Peel himself was convinced that repeal was essential. In 1846, the threat of a famine in Ireland following the failure of the potato crop provided him with the excuse he needed. Peel skilfully exploited the Irish issue, claiming that cheap grain was needed in order to save four million Irish men, women and children from 'the calamity of starvation'.[4] On June 26th 1846 Parliament repealed the Corn Laws. In this act of repeal, the new economic order was sealed and the middle classes had affirmed their control of the economic agenda.

5 The Early Railway Age

In 1830, the world's first passenger railway, between Liverpool and Manchester, was opened. As a feat of engineering, the line was an impressive achievement, though the real significance lay in the economic implications of the transport revolution which followed. By 1850, over 6,000 miles of track had been laid and the 'railway age' had arrived. The immediate success of the 30-mile line between Liverpool and Manchester stimulated a railway investment boom which demonstrated the ability of Victorian business to generate vast sums of money, necessary to finance this construction programme. Speculative investment in the railways peaked in the 'railway manias' of 1839-40 and 1845-47. The results of this investment is apparent on the map on page 51.

The railway became the symbol of Victorian industrial and technical ingenuity. So why did the railway age begin?

a) Supply Factors

The steam railway was essentially the result of two major technical advances. The ability to produce the necessary quantities of high-quality, low-cost wrought-iron rails, as a result of the technical advances outlined in the previous chapter (see page 23), made the construction of the railways a viable proposition. Secondly, the technical advances in steam-engine technology, allowing steam locomotion, is equally important. The first steam locomotives, most notably Richard Trevithick's *Catch Me Who Can* (1808), William Hedley's

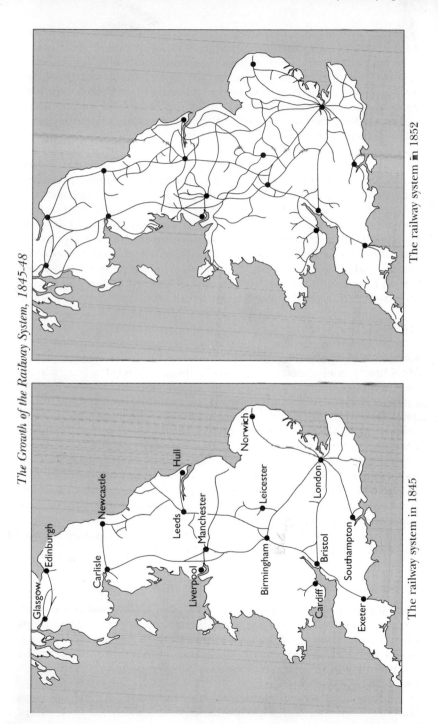

The Growth of the Railway System, 1845–48

The railway system in 1845

The railway system in 1852

Glasgow
Edinburgh
Newcastle
Carlisle
Liverpool
Leeds
Hull
Manchester
Leicester
Norwich
Birmingham
London
Cardiff
Bristol
Southampton
Exeter

Puffing Billy (1813) and George Stephenson's *Blucher* (1814), all suffered from technical inadequacies. The low speeds of around 4 mph, limited power, and a tendency to break down regularly ensured that early locomotives were not a serious alternative to road or canal transport. In the late 1820s, however, improved models emerged, many of which were displayed at the Rainhill Trials, on the Liverpool to Manchester Railway in 1829. This competition, held to decide which locomotives would work the new railway, was won by George Stephenson's *Rocket*, which achieved a top speed of 27 mph and demonstrated greater reliability than its rivals.

The Liverpool to Manchester Railway proved an immediate success and, at once, was followed by other railway schemes which saw the major British towns and cities linked by rail by the mid century.

The enormous cost of the railways, on average £40,000 per mile, was met from two main sources. The most significant source was the issue of shares by the railway companies. Shares were available to the general public, with the middle class in particular heavily involved in railway investment. Between 1828 and 1844, an estimated 45 per cent of shares were bought by merchants, 28 per cent by the landed classes, 11 per cent by manufacturers, 9 per cent by the professions and 5 per cent by women. Although some inexperienced investors had their fingers burned in speculative schemes, the trunk routes proved to be lucrative to shareholders. It is due to the fact that the middle class in particular held surplus capital that railway construction on such a scale was possible. The newly emerging joint-stock banks also invested considerable sums, accounting for 37 per cent of total railway investment before 1850. In the 50 years between 1825 and 1875, £630 million was invested in British railways, far in excess of investment in any other single industry.

The British civil-engineering industry rose to the challenge of railway construction admirably. The canal building programme had created the necessary skills base, which was developed by the great railway engineers including, amongst others, George Stephenson and, most famously, Isambard Kingdom Brunel. The technical achievements of such men astounded contemporaries and set new standards in civil engineering.

b) Demand Factors

The rapid expansion of the rail network indicates the existence of an economic need for improvements to Britain's transport system. In this respect the following extract from the *Prospectus of the Liverpool and Manchester Railroad Company*, published in 1824, provides useful insight into the views of contemporary businessmen:

I   Railroads are now proposed to be established. ... as means of conveyance manifestly superior to existing modes. ... The railroad

scheme holds out to the public not only a cheaper, but far more expe-
ditious conveyance than any yet established. The importance, to a
5 commercial state, of a safe and cheap mode of transit for merchandise,
from one part of the country to another, will be readily acknowledged.
The total quantity of merchandise passing between Liverpool and
Manchester is estimated, by the lowest computation, at 1,000 tons per
day. The bulk of this merchandise is transported either by the Duke of
10 Bridgewater's Canal, or the 'Mersey and Irwell Navigation'. By both of
these conveyances goods must pass up the river Mersey, a distance of
16 or 18 miles, subject to serious delays from contrary winds, and not
infrequently, to actual loss or damage from tempestuous weather. The
average length of passage, by these conveyances, including the
15 customary detention on the wharves, may be taken at 36 hours. ... The
average charge upon merchandise for the last 14 years has been about
15s. per ton.
By the projected railroad, the transit of merchandise between
Liverpool and Manchester will be effected in four or five hours, and
20 the charge to the merchant will be reduced at least one-third.
Here, then, will be accomplished an immense pecuniary saving to
the public, over and above what is perhaps still more important,
the economy of time. ... It will afford stimulus to the productive
industry of the country; it will give a new impulse to the powers
25 of accumulation, the value and importance of which can be fully understood only by those who are aware how seriously commerce may be
impeded by petty restrictions, and how commercial enterprise is
encouraged and promoted by an adherence to the principles of fair
competition and free trade.
30 ... It is not that the water companies have not been able to carry
goods on more reasonable terms, but that, strong in the enjoyment of
their monopoly, they have not thought proper to do so. ... IT IS
COMPETITION THAT IS WANTED. ...
But it is not altogether an account of the exorbitant charges of the
35 water-carriers that a railroad is desirable. The present canal establish-
ments are inadequate to ... the regular and punctual conveyance of
goods at all periods and seasons. In summer time there is frequently a
deficiency of water, obliging boats to go only half loaded. ... While, in
winter, they are sometimes locked up with frosts, for weeks together'.[5]

The continued expansion of industry and the potential for passenger
transport clearly stimulated railway growth. The railway quickly established a reputation as a mode of transport which was a great improvement on canals, especially in terms of speed and, crucially, cost.
It is estimated that, on average, the early railways undercut canals by
10 per cent or more on passenger fares and by 30 per cent on freight.
Efficiency, competitiveness and technical progress ensured that the
railway was rapidly embraced by British business. Its impact, discussed
in Chapter 4, was indeed profound.

All this was achieved with little government involvement, and the role of the State remained secondary to that of the private companies. Parliamentary approval was, however, required for each new scheme, and from 1840 a Railway Department was set up within the Board of Trade, especially concerned with safety issues. In 1844 the Railways Act ensured that at least one train per day provided third-class accommodation in each direction at no more than one penny per mile (creating what became known as the parliamentary trains). This helped open up rail traffic to the masses, though more significant government involvement occurred after 1850 when the amalgamation of rail companies, forming regional monopolies and therefore damaging competition, resulted in closer government scrutiny of the industry. For the most part, the railway sector, as with British industry generally, developed according to market forces.

6 Social Responses to Industrialisation

For all the economic progress so far outlined from the industrial revolution onwards, we should not lose sight of the fact that industrialisation also had its social costs. The expansion of the industrial town impacted upon health standards, seriously affecting the environmental quality of the surroundings of the working class. As the impact of urbanisation, mechanisation and industrial growth were felt, so voices of dissent were increasingly heard. Many among the working classes of Britain were moved to voice their discontent through political protest, trades union activity and, at times, riot and violence.

A major source of discontent was the level of poverty that existed, particularly amongst the lesser skilled. In times of recession they became the first economic victims, as a downturn in trade resulted in job losses or short-time working. For the hundreds of thousands of men employed in 'casual' labour, such as dock workers or labourers in the construction industry, who were taken on a daily basis as and when work was available, there was great uncertainty in employment. The recession of 1837-42 proved to be especially harsh, significantly boosting the numbers of unemployed. During this recession, which hit the cotton-textile trade especially hard, unemployment in Bolton, for example, reached 60 per cent in 1842. In the construction trades in the same town, unemployment peaked at 87 per cent of workers in that sector. Amongst the dockers of Liverpool, just over 50 per cent were out of work as trade slumped. The absence of adequate financial assistance to the poor was exacerbated by the reform of the Poor Law, as the 1834 Poor Law Amendment Act had blocked the payment of 'outdoor relief' (direct money payment) to the able-bodied poor.

Some contemporary observers, such as the philosopher and historian Thomas Carlyle, believed that the increase in mechanisation had materially worsened the lives of the poor. Lamenting this development, he claimed in 1829 that:

> It is the age of the machine. ... Nothing now is done directly, - or by
> hand. Old modes of exertion are discredited and thrown aside. ... On
> every hand, the living artisan is driven from his workshop, to make room
> for a speedier, inanimate one.[6]

Whilst this represents an extreme and exaggerated view of what was
happening, in some sectors, such as handloom weaving, workers
were thrown into severe poverty. Mechanisation, factory conditions,
the length of the working day, and low pay represented the concerns
of the urban, industrial working classes. The gloomy life of the
factory operative thus became a focus of criticism, with the factory
master often presented as the perpetrator of the exploitation of his
workforce. The worker found an ally in the form of Parliament,
which legislated in 1833, 1844 and 1847 to set a minimum age at
which children could work in the factories and restrict the length of
the working day. In 1842, the Mines Act took women and children
out of the pit. Workers in these industries also took steps to protect
themselves against the worst excesses of industrialisation. Fear of
unemployment or reduced wages swelled the ranks of working-class
movements. Trades unions, often led by socialist-inspired radicals,
led the fight to protect and improve wages and reduce hours. Yet
poor communications, strong employer resistance to strikes and the
financial weaknesses of unions and their members, severely restricted
union success, especially amongst the semi-skilled or unskilled
workers. By the late 1840s, union membership totalled around
100,000; an insignificant proportion of the national workforce. Many
more workers turned to the co-operative movement as a more
practical means whereby, through self-help, working people were
able directly to address their pressing need for access to cheap, better
quality food.

Chartism proved to be the most significant political response of the
masses to times of crisis. Often seen as a protest movement, enjoying
widespread support only in times of crisis, Chartism demanded political representation for the working classes by extending the vote to all
men over 21. Only through radical reform of both Parliament and the
outdated voting system, the Chartist leaders believed, could the social
problems of the working classes be resolved. Yet the strong resistance
by government to Chartism, the inherent weaknesses of the movement itself and the improving economic climate by the end of the
1840s all ensured Chartism did not succeed.

Such movements clearly demonstrate that the industrial revolution
had not brought with it unqalified progress. The economic gains of
industrialisation were, of course, unequally distributed. We are uncer-
tain of the impact of industrial growth on living standards. It is essential
to consider a broad range of factors in assessing whether or not the
people as a whole were better off as the economy grew. We know that,
in overall terms, money wages did improve in the first half of the

nineteenth century. However, the question of living standards is not so simple. To what extent was a rise in wages countered by urban over-crowding, the growth of slums, the presence of epidemic disease (such as cholera in 1832 and 1848), rising death rates, unemployment and poor working conditions, to name but a few? Increasing emigration, especially to North America, Australia and New Zealand, would suggest that hundreds of thousands believed that the prospect of a better future lay in foreign parts.

In rural areas the poor fared no better. The continued growth of the rural population increased competition for work during a time of stagnation. This, coupled with lower agricultural prices, depressed wage levels. At the same time the rural labourer, whose wages compared unfavourably with his urban industrial counterpart, was forced to pay the same price for food and was still vulnerable to price rises in years of poor harvests. The decline of rural industry, such as that of woollen textiles in Norfolk, further harmed rural labourers. Nevertheless, the rural labourer demonstrated a surprising reluct-ance to migrate. Britain did not witness the mass depopulation of the countryside in favour of urban employment. Distress in rural Britain remained a feature of the 30 years after the Napoleonic wars. Petty crime, especially poaching, did increase, despite the draconian penalties handed down by the courts. Rioting and violence caused by economic distress in East Anglia in 1816 resulted in the execution of five men and the transportation of ten others. The problem of distress in rural Britain reached a climax in 1830 with serious rioting across southern England. The introduction of threshing machines provoked a bitter response from a labour force already suffering severe hardship. Nineteen hangings and over 500 transportations crushed what became known as the last labourers' revolt, though repressive action did nothing to diminish the causes of unrest.

7 Assessment

Despite the clear social difficulties facing the nation, the overall picture indicates an economy enjoying growth as Britain entered a new phase of industrialisation. Total output of the economy, valued at £340 million in 1831, had reached £523 million 20 years later. Export values doubled in the same period, whilst prices for the main exports of cotton and woollen textiles had actually fallen, empha-sising the exceptional export performance of these industries. Furthermore, as the size of the population was increasing at over 15 per cent per decade, industrial growth was creating new jobs to absorb most of this increase. Despite, then, the sluggish per-formance of the economy in the post-war years and the serious recession of 1839-43, the British economy continued on the path of industrialisation.

References

1   A. Aspinall and E.A. Smith (eds), *English Historical Documents*, Vol. XI (Oxford University Press, 1959), p. 557.
2   Ibid, p. 563.
3   Asa Briggs, *The Age of Improvement* (Longman, 1966), p. 214.
4   G.M. Young and W.D. Handcock (eds), *English Historical Documents*, Vol. XII (Oxford University Press, 1959), p. 456.
5   Aspinall and Smith (eds), *English Historical Documents*, Vol. XI, pp. 546-7.
6   Richard Brown, *Economic Revolution in Britain 1750-1850* (Cambridge University Press, 1992), p.49.

Answering essay questions on 'The Development of the Industrial Economy c. 1815-50'

Consider the following:

1. What, in your view, were the positive and negative results of industrialisation for the nation and its people by 1851?
2. What were the main arguments in favour of free trade, and why were they so widely accepted by 1850?
3.

Growth of Towns, 1821-51
(Figures of population in thousands)

	1821	1831	1841	1851
Bath	47	51	53	54
Birmingham	102	144	183	233
Liverpool	138	202	286	376
Glasgow	147	202	275	345
Norwich	50	61	62	68
Preston	25	34	51	70

Outline and explain the trends in urban population growth demonstrated in the table above.

You might compile two separate lists in answering question 1. Remember, there may be positive and negative social results. Similarly, economic outcomes were not always positive. Questions 2 and 3 are more challenging. Here we have two very different types of question. Remember that your first task is to be absolutely sure what the question requires. Each demands an introduction in which you will need to demonstrate an awareness of the context of the question. In your introduction to question 2, you may wish to demonstrate an awareness of the origins of the free-trade debate and the time-scale of the move towards free trade. In your introduction to question 3, on

Summary Diagram
The Development of the Industrial Economy c. 1815-50

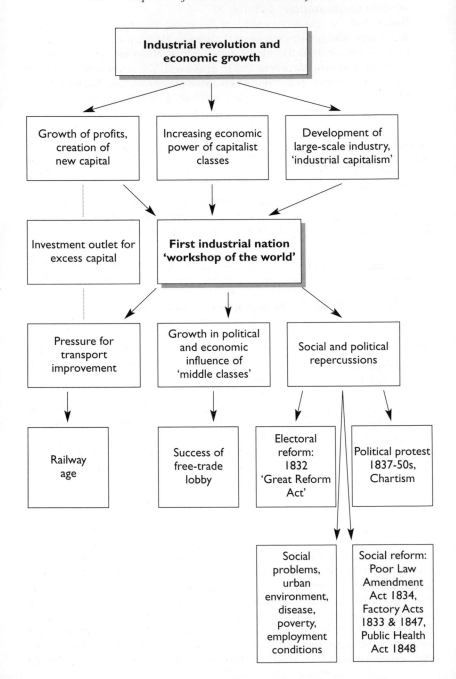

the other hand, you might outline to the reader the point that the growth of the cities shown was part of a general growth of the total population of the nation at that time.

In devising the main structure of the essay, you will find that question 2 poses few problems. There are two very specific issues to be addressed and your answers to these questions constitute the main body of the essay. Stick to the point, and avoid the temptation to drift into a narrative on the Anti-Corn-Law League or the opposition to free trade.

Question 3 is more problematic and, when constructing your answer, you might consider why the particular cities shown have been chosen. What was the economic function of each city between the dates shown? What effect was economic growth having on that particular function? How does the rate of growth differ between cities? What was the geographical location of the city?

The material relevant to question 2 can be located in the text of this chapter. Question 3, however, will require you to base your answer on ideas developed throughout the book so far.

Source-based questions on 'The Development of the Industrial Economy c. 1815-50'

1. The Growth of the Iron Industry, 1820-49

Examine the statistical data relating to the production and value of pig iron on page 43. Answer the following questions:

a) What were the consequences for the iron industry of the relative changes in the production of pig iron and the value of pig iron produced between 1820 and 1849? (2 marks)
b) Account for these changes. (4 marks)
c) Using the data provided and your own knowledge, assess the contribution of the iron industry to British industrial growth in the period between 1820 and 1849. (8 marks)
d) What are the limitations of the figures provided as evidence relating to the expansion of the iron industry in this period? (6 marks)

Hints and advice

The views and theories of economic historians are often based on the sort of statistical data presented by this question. The skill of interpreting such material is, therefore, one that you will need to develop. Often there is no exact answer to the sort of questions set above. Inferences and informed speculation are to be encouraged! It is essential, though, that you don't try and read too much into the data. Production figures and values can only tell us so much. What don't they tell us which we may need to know to fully appreciate, for example, the causes of the growth of production? On the other hand, you should also be aware that statistics provide more than a simple snapshot of individual years. What happens to production in iron can tell us much of what was happening in the broader economic environment. Look for trends in the figures. Are there any obvious booms or slumps, for example? From your knowledge of other areas of industry, how do the fortunes of iron fit in with the macro-economic picture?

2. The Prospectus of the Liverpool and Manchester Railroad Company

Examine the extract from the document on pages 52 and 53. Answer the following questions:

a) What was the purpose of the prospectus? (2 marks)
b) What, does the prospectus suggest, were the advantages presented by a railway between Liverpool and Manchester, over existing modes of transport? (8 marks)
c) From your own knowledge explain why efficient transport links between the two cities were so important at this time. (2 marks)
d) How does the prospectus reflect the prevailing business doctrines of the day? (4 marks)
e) What, in your view, are the weaknesses of the extract as evidence relating to the desirability of a rail link between Liverpool and Manchester? (4 marks)

Hints and advice
The key to fully understanding this extract is to appreciate the inter-relationship between increasing levels of industrialisation and growth of the railway network from 1830 to 1850. Questions (a) and (b) deal with the perceived need for transport improvements and this calls for some knowledge of the faults and deficiencies of existing transport options. Question (c) develops the point further by calling for an understanding of the role of both cities in British industrialisation. Clearly, with eight marks at stake, question (b) calls for the closest attention. Of the first three questions, it is the only one that requires a full analysis of the text. Ensure that you don't simply rewrite the text. Examiners do not like this! Neither is it what the question demands. Far better to identify what the promoters of this scheme saw as the likely benefits. Can you demonstrate an understanding of their motivation in proposing the railway? This point links effectively with question (d). Apart from the improvements to the physical movement of goods, how would the railway promote a healthier business climate? Who were the promoters of the scheme? In question (e) there is a need to develop this point, by clearly stating that those responsible for the prospectus have a specific agenda. They need to win financial support for the railway. Is the prospectus presenting a balanced assessment of the need for a railway? Is there bias that needs to be highlighted?

4 The Zenith of British Economic Power, 1851-73

1 Mid-Victorian Prosperity

By the mid nineteenth century, Britain was clearly reaping the rewards of industrialisation, becoming the most powerful economy in the world. The years 1851-73 witnessed the zenith of British industrial and economic power. Surging production levels, most notably in cotton textiles, iron and steel, coal mining and engineering, were critical to British domination of the global economy. The claim, which has become a cliché of economic history, that during this period, Britain became the 'Workshop of the World' remains valid. However, it is the pace of the development of the economy and the extent of Britain's domination of the world economy achieved during these years which makes this period unique. Britain became the world's most powerful economy because of the wealth the staple industries created. However, this was accompanied by the development of a more broadly-based economy. The engineering sector in particular diversified, providing a broadening range of products, creating thousands of jobs and earning millions of pounds in markets both at home and abroad. Shipbuilding, machine making, steam-engine production and the products associated with railway construction were increasingly vital to economic growth.

Successive generations of economic historians have recognised the impressive dynamism of the British economy during this period, and the performance of the industrial sector has been subjected to intense scrutiny in attempts to explain the emergence of the world's first industrial economy. Most famously, perhaps, R.A. Church has described the years 1851-73 as 'The Great Victorian Boom',[1] whilst that doyen of left-wing economic historians, E.J. Hobsbawm, wrote of an economic transformation between 1848 and the early 1870s which was 'so extraordinary that men were lost for a precedent.'[2] Peter Mathias claimed that, from 1851, British economic supremacy was such that 'never before and never since has one country so dominated the world economy'[3] and that 'as Britain assumed this dominant role in the international economy, exploiting the unique advantages of a unique position, so the prime dynamic in the economy became the industrial sector, and within that, directly and indirectly, the export industries.'[4] More recently R.C. Floud, in supporting the idea of a period of unprecedented economic well-being, observed that between 1850 and 1873 'prosperity extended across all forms of economic activity, from foreign trade to farming and its benefits were diffused throughout the British population.'[5]

Growth rates show a steady expansion of the economy for the period as a whole, although this growth was more pronounced at certain times than others.

Estimated Economic Growth Rates (Per annum average)	
1847-53	3.5%
1854-60	1.7%
1861-65	3.6%
1866-74	2.1%

National income enjoyed a corresponding growth, with per capita figures increasing from £22.9 in 1855 to £33.9 in 1875, a significant increase, although of course such figures can disguise enormous disparities between the various income groups. Nevertheless the figures represent considerable growth.

The principal aim of this chapter is to establish the factual basis for the claim that this was a unique period in British economic history. It will consider the nature and extent of economic and industrial development and outline the factors which created unprecedented levels of national wealth. These include the accelerated growth of the staple industries; the accrued benefits of the railway network; the growth of international trade; the development of the financial sector; and the improved fortunes of agriculture.

a) Contemporary Opinion

By the mid century, the manufacturing and commercial middle classes of Britain were keenly aware of the growing economic and industrial strength of the nation and of the opportunities which lay ahead. The ethos of economic liberalism - the freeing of commercial activity from political intervention - inspired the men of free enterprise. The anticipated benefits of free trade, in particular boosting export opportunities (see page 77), were seen by contemporaries as critical to future development. Industrial capitalism, free from the shackles of protectionism, became the new economic orthodoxy. Although complete freedom from import duties had not yet been achieved, the level of duties on a small number of imported goods was very low and in the following decade most of the few remaining tariffs were swept away. The confidence inspired by the success of the free-trade lobby is well illustrated by the words of Absolom Watkin, an active campaigner for free trade and ex-Anti-Corn-Law Leaguer, who recorded in his diary in 1853, that 'Never have I seen clearer evidence of general well-being. Our country is, no doubt, in a most happy and prosperous state; Free Trade, peace and freedom.'[6]

The great industrial centres continued their rapid rate of growth and, as a consequence, the urban population accounted for 65 per cent of the population in 1871, compared to 54 per cent in 1851. This expansion exacerbated the social problems of overcrowding, poverty and high death rates, denounced by the likes of Friedrich Engels as an abomination resulting from the worst excesses of industrial capitalism. Such negative accounts of the state of inner-city Britain were undoubtedly justified in terms of the shocking state of many working-class districts. However, industrial cities such as Manchester also inspired awe at the wealth-generating capacities of its industries. To the commercial mind of the mid nineteenth century, such cities were the epitome of human progress, as the following extracts from contemporary publications testify:

1 This city - this great capital of the weavers and spinners of the earth, the Manchester of the power loom, the Manchester of the League, *our* Manchester - is but a thing of yesterday. A man, only a few years dead, recollected the people crowding to admire the first tall chimney built in
5 Manchester, and had seen the Liverpool coach set forth at six in the morning, in good hope of reaching its destination not very long after six o'clock at night. Considerably within two thirds of a century, the scattered villages of Manchester, Salford, Hulme, Pendleton, Chorlton and two or three others, became the vast cotton metropolis which has
10 lately succeeded in swaying the industrial and commercial polity of England.[7]

  Manchester streets may be irregular, and its trading inscriptions pretentious, its smoke may be dense and its mud ultra muddy, but not any or all of these things can prevent the image of a great city rising
15 before us as the very symbol of civilisation, foremost in the march of improvement, a grand incarnation of progress.[8]

Even appalling living conditions, it seems, had their compensations!

  This sense of progress and success must have seemed well founded. In 1851, British mills manufactured 55 per cent of the world's cotton cloth, its foundries 50 per cent of the world's iron and 65 per cent of its steel. British miners produced 65 per cent of the world's coal. Britain completely eclipsed its closest rivals in terms of railway mileage and built most of its iron ships and steam engines. In addition, a fifth of all products transported on the high seas between nations were en route to or from a British port. The political crises of the 1830s and 1840s had been superseded by a period of relative social stability and in 1851 Britain was on the verge of a great economic and industrial age. She would remain without serious challenge for a quarter of a century.

b) The Great Exhibition and Census of 1851

The central importance of the manufacturing industries to the nation was clearly demonstrated at the Great Exhibition of 1851. In effect, the Exhibition was the British response to a less ambitious industrial exhibition held in Paris in 1849 and was the world's first trade fair. The 'Great Exhibition of the Works of Industry of All Nations', opened by Prince Albert, was held in the Crystal Palace, a building specifically designed and created for the purpose. Civil servant and organiser of the exhibition, Henry Cole, proclaimed that 'A great people invited all civilised nations to a festival, to bring into comparison the works of human skill.' In reality, however, this event was an unashamed demonstration to the world of British industrial and technical supremacy. Over half of the 13,000 exhibitors and 100,000 exhibits were of British or Empire origin. The exhibition was a manifestation of the optimism of the times and, in particular, the progress of the nation. Around six million visitors, of all classes, witnessed at first hand the success of industrial capitalism promoted here as a vehicle of human progress. G.R. Porter, a contemporary statistician with the Board of Trade, claimed in 1851, in his work *Progress of the Nation From the Beginning of the Nineteenth Century*, that 'The capital, skill and energy possessed and exercised by the inhabitants of these islands will, when unfettered, carry us forward to a degree of commercial and manufacturing prosperity of which the world has hitherto seen no example.'

Yet not all opinion was so supportive of the idea of industrial capitalism as the harbinger of progress. The cartoon, from *Punch* magazine (see over leaf), suggested in 1850 that the progress of the nation and capitalism had not been an unqualified success.

The image of a nation at the forefront of industrial and technological progress, so confidently proclaimed at the Great Exhibition, should be seen in perspective. The official census of 1851 provides historians with a useful snapshot of certain aspects of the economic and social make-up of the nation. As the first modern and reliable census to offer a survey of the population, the figures actually reveal a nation whose economy was still heavily dependent upon non-factory-based employment, relying on minimal levels of technology. In employment terms, traditional activities such as agriculture, unskilled labouring work and the old crafts still predominated. Workers in factories, mines and foundries were in the minority.

In terms of aggregate figures, iron and steel languished in seventeenth place, with 80,000 employed in this sector, whereas there were

Principal Forms of Occupation by Size of Workforce in 1851 (To nearest thousand)			
Occupation	Total	Occupation	Total
Agriculture	1,790,000	Milliner, dressmaker	340,000
Domestic service	1,039,000	Wool worker (includes	
Cotton worker (includes		domestic & processing)	284,000
domestic & processing)	527,000	Shoemaker	274,000
Building trades	443,000	Coal miner	219,000
Labourer (general)	376,000	Tailor	153,000

SPECIMENS FROM MR. PUNCH'S INDUSTRIAL EXHIBITION OF 1850.

A *Punch* cartoon

still 113,000 traditional blacksmiths. The railways employed 65,000 as drivers and porters, whilst 84,000 found employment in the road transport sector as carter, coachman and cabby. Nevertheless, it is true to say that the following 20 years witnessed an increasing shift towards a more technologically-based industrial sector, and an increasing proportion of the workforce found work in factories.

2 The Staple Industries as the Vanguard of Economic Growth

The role of coal, cotton textiles and the iron and steel industries was central to the success of the British economy in this period. Continued expansion of production, investment and employment in these sectors feature prominently in the mid-Victorian period. In the early 1850s, they accounted for 56 per cent of exports by value and employed over 800,000 workers. By the mid 1870s, despite the growth of other export sectors, particularly engineering, their share of exports was still 53 per cent, employing just over one million workers. A short examination of the main developments in coal, cotton textiles, iron and steel and engineering not only indicates their strength, but also aids our understanding of the nature of British economic development.

a) Coal

Coal was the single most important industrial fuel. Its production figures therefore provide a useful measure of the general industrial climate. Changing consumption patterns of coal tell us a good deal of what was happening in the economy. Coal consumption can usefully be broken down into six main areas: general manufacturing, metal industries, transport, domestic use, exports and for use in the mines themselves (to power steam pumps to keep the mines free from flooding). In all these areas there was a considerable growth in demand. Indeed so great was this increase that production levels doubled, with important consequences for employment.

Production and Employment in British Coal Mines, 1851-73		
Year	Estimated Production (Million tons)	Estimated Numbers Employed
1851	65.2	216,200
1855	76.4	242,700
1861	89.2	282,500
1865	102.3	315,500
1871	121.4	370,900
1873	128.0	465,200

The steady growth in coal production outlined here was mirrored by the growth of the industry's principal customers. The ability of the coal industry to meet the increasing demand ensured that British industrial development was not held back by fuel considerations. Of the six sources of demand outlined above, the most significant in quantitative terms came from general manufacturing. The need for direct heat in industries such as brickmaking and brewing, and for raising steam in the growing number of companies using steam power, resulted in a growth in consumption in this sector from an estimated 18 million tons in 1855 to 30 million tons in 1869. For the metal industries the figures rose from 15 to 26 million tons, for domestic consumption from 15 million tons to 19 million, while exports rose to 10 million. The mines themselves required 7 million tons in 1869 to fuel the steam pumps, compared with only 4 million tons in 1855. The increases in consumption are all the more remarkable when it is remembered that, in the metal trades and for steam engines, the period witnessed improvements which had actually resulted in fuel economies due to more efficient technologies.

The coal industry successfully met the growth in demand as entrepreneurs opened more mines, exploited more seams and employed more men. Improved winding gear, improved ventilation techniques and control of water levels had made mines safer and contributed to some growth in productivity. Deeper shafts could now be sunk and thus previously unobtainable coal reserves became available. In the 1830s, shafts of a depth of 1,000 feet were exceptional; in the 1860s, however, shafts of this depth were the norm, and some were twice as deep. Partly as a result of these developments, output increased from a national average of 231 tons per man per year in 1850 to 315 tons in 1870. The industry was able to increase overall profits, particularly in the booms of 1854-56, 1864-66 and 1871-73. Some individuals fared particularly well, the Earl of Durham increasing his annual earnings from his mining interests from £70,000 in 1838 to £380,000 in 1873. Heavy demand, cheap labour and readily accessible reserves of coal encouraged investment. Profits were healthy overall, with the combined profits of the industry reaching £7.2 million in 1873, compared with £2.8 million in 1870, although this also reflects a short-term price boom in those years.

This apparently prosperous picture should not, however, be simply accepted without some qualifications, not least on the issue of productivity. Admittedly there were improvements in comparison with earlier periods, but it must be remembered that low levels of productivity from earlier years give an exaggerated impression of productivity gains in the mid-Victorian era. Pick and shovel remained the principal form of coal extraction, and in the relatively easily won seams of the huge Northumberland coalfield and the emerging coalmining region of South Wales it was not difficult to improve productivity as large-scale reserves were discovered and developed. The relative lack of mechanisation in British pits made economic sense to mine owners. Coal-cutting technology was in its infancy and not always suited to British mines, particularly in those areas such as the Lancashire coalfield where the seams were narrow. Furthermore, the availability of a large pool of cheap labour reduced the incentive to invest in technology. The organisation of the coal industry in Britain also acted as a bar to large-scale capital investment. The predominant form of ownership remained the single entrepreneur owning one or a small number of pits. There was no tradition of large-scale joint-stock companies controlling the industry. As a result, few mine owners were able to afford heavy capital investment.

This point raises a serious issue other than that of low productivity. A lack of capital investment was a contributory factor to the high number of deaths in British mines.

Total Deaths Recorded in British Coal Mines from Accidents		
Years	Total Deaths	Average per Year
1851-55	985	197.0
1856-60	1,018	235.4
1861-65	967	193.4
1866-70	1,158	231.6
1871-75	1,101	220.2

These figures, however, must be seen in the light of the growing numbers employed. They clearly suggest that overall, although still inherently dangerous, coalmining was in fact becoming safer. It should also be noted that there were great regional disparities, with fatalities in the more difficult regions being higher than in the safer coalfields. In the Northumberland and Durham coalfield, for instance, the death rate of miners from accidents was 1.9 per thousand employed in 1870. In the more geologically complex Lancashire coalfield, the rate was 3.3 per thousand. However, the national average did improve, with deaths from accidents declining from 4 per thousand employed in 1855 to half that figure in 1875. Furthermore, general mortality rates amongst coalminers were lower than those for less well-paid occupations, with agricultural labourers, general labourers and construction workers having higher rates than coalminers, despite the respiratory problems associated with coalmining.

b) Cotton Textiles

The history of the cotton-textile industry in this period is also one of expansion and prosperity. It strengthened its position as a leading sector of the economy. Productivity improvements continued at an average of 2.1 per cent per annum in the spinning sector, and 2.7 per cent in weaving. Although the great inventions and innovation had taken place in earlier decades of the nineteenth century, the mechanisation of both spinning and weaving continued. Even the more widespread adoption of steam power and of the application of ever larger steam engines, spinning mules and looms increased productivity. At the same time, the combined spinning and weaving mill was superseded as manufacturers exploited a growing market by specialising in one branch of the trade.

The buoyant state of the industry may be seen through the scale of employment, most of which was concentrated in Lancashire.

As in the coal industry, the small-scale employer still predominated, with the ownership by an individual of a single mill being typical. Although over the course of the period the average size of a spinning mill rose from 105.7 employees in 1850 to 123.5 in 1873, the average mill in 1873 still resembled more closely that of the mill of the 1820s than that of the new generation of mills built at the turn of the twentieth century, which employed over 1,000 workers. In the mid-Victorian period there was still scope for the small, privately-owned firm. Relatively small-scale capital investment was still worthwhile, given booming market conditions in which profit was almost assured. Cotton-mill ownership still provided status, influence and power. For these reasons, the family firm thrived, aided by the fact that there was, as yet, no shift towards joint-stock ownership. Even the hand loom weaver retained a precarious presence in the industry with an estimated 10,000 operating in the late 1850s until their final demise in the following decade.

Total production levels rose impressively in response to rocketing demand. The growth of the export sector provided the greatest spur to production, accounting for 60 per cent of total sales in 1871.

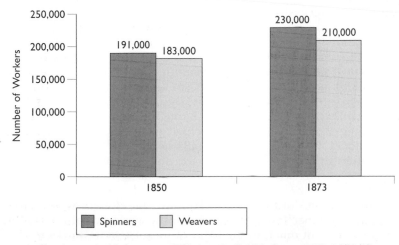

Employment of Spinners and Weavers in British Cotton Mills 1850-73

In those areas where climatic conditions demanded a lightweight cloth, and where relatively high poverty levels demanded a low-price product, cotton held obvious advantages over competing products such as wool or silk. Consequently, the growth of Asian markets, most notably India and China and Latin America, where Brazil dominated the market, outstripped traditional export destinations including Europe and the USA. In the latter case, a strong domestic industry developed, based on a home-produced raw material, an expanding domestic market and the increased use of tariffs against British cotton cloth. Europe too began to develop domestic production, with the German states also raising tariffs to protect their fledgling textile sector. India became critical to the Lancashire cotton industry at this time, being by far the largest single market. As Farnie claimed, 'The growth of exports to India transformed the pattern of Anglo-Indian trade and provided the British empire with a new economic base'.[9] The export of finished cloth to India accounted for 16.6 per cent of total cloth by value produced in Britain in 1851. This had reached 19.4 per cent in 1873.

The profit of cotton textiles in these years is not, however, one of uninterrupted growth. The 'Cotton Famine' of 1862-65 is traditionally interpreted as having a devastating effect upon the Lancashire cotton industry. The closure of Lancashire textile mills or the use of short-time working has been explained by the slump in exports of raw cotton to Britain as union forces blockaded southern United States ports from the beginning of the American Civil War in 1861. However, historians have challenged this assertion and it is no longer acceptable for students to perpetuate this simplistic version of events. Although there is no doubt that vast stocks of raw cotton remained stranded on the quaysides of southern ports, the actual impact upon the Lancashire cotton trade has been exaggerated. Mill owners and merchants were cushioned from the full impact of this disruption to supplies for a number of reasons. Firstly, large stocks of unsold cotton cloth had built up over 1859-61 as a short-term crisis in India, resulting from drought and famine, had resulted in a slump in sales to that market. Large quantities of cloth thus remained unsold. Mill owners and merchants could therefore cut production and still have cloth to sell. Secondly, the rise in raw-material prices, which resulted from the war in the United States, discouraged many mill owners from buying. They decided to sit out the crisis, selling excess stocks and reducing wage bills by severely cutting hours of work, often operating the factory for no more than two days per week, relying on existing raw cotton or yarn stocks to see them through.

The real victims of the 'Cotton Famine' therefore were the workforce. In November 1862, 20 per cent of the workforce of Lancashire were recipients of relief, in the form of soup kitchens, work-creation schemes and other forms of charitable provision. In towns where cotton mills were the principal employers, conditions were especially difficult, with widespread distress apparent. In Preston, a town where 50 per cent of the adult population worked in the mills in 1862, 30 per cent of the total population in December of that year depended upon relief for survival.

By 1865 the crisis was over as markets recovered and the American Civil War ended, and the industry rapidly recovered to former levels of production. In the longer term, only those firms working to the tightest of financial margins failed to survive.

c) Iron and Steel and Engineering

The provision of high-quality, low-price iron and steel was a continuing feature of industrial expansion. The development of the railways, great civil-engineering projects and the revolution in the mechanical and light-engineering sectors - were only possible because of the iron and steel industry's ability to meet demand. To contemporaries, the age of iron and steel, together with advances in engineering, represented a new technological age, with Britain at the forefront of progress.

As in the case of coal and cotton textiles, production levels in the iron and steel sectors soared. Investment in new plant, in response to demand and technological breakthrough, resulted in a huge growth in the capacity of the industry. Bigger and more fuel-efficient furnaces produced cheap iron. The exploitation of new reserves of iron ore in Lincolnshire, Cleveland and southern Lakeland resulted in the emergence of new industrial towns such as Middlesborough (which quadrupled its population in the third quarter of the century) and Barrow-in-Furness.

Technological advance was most pronounced in the steel sector, especially after the development of the Bessemer Converter in 1856. Henry Bessemer devised a method whereby a blast of hot air into a converter containing molten pig iron allowed for the production of cheaper steel by driving out impurities in the molten iron. The addition of small amounts of manganese, a process pioneered by Robert Mushet, ensured that the brittleness of the resulting steel was significantly reduced. Cheap, high-quality steel became available, provided non-phosphoric ores were used. In Britain, the major source of such ore was in the Barrow-in-Furness region, although increasingly Spanish ores were imported to meet demand. The cost of steel fell rapidly. Costing £50 per ton in 1850, 20 years later the price had fallen to between £3 and £4 per ton.

The engineering sector, in its many forms, developed ever more complex skills, achieving a range of major technological advances and transforming some sectors of engineering. The great civil-engineering projects of this time, not least the railways, the advent of the inter-

Iron and Steel Production in Britain, 1850-73		
Pig iron produced	1850	3,000,000 tons
	1873	6,300,000 tons
Steel produced	1850	60,000 tons
	1873	700,000 tons

national telegraph system and even the provision of sewers in Britain's great cities transformed more than the physical appearance of the nation. Similarly, the mechanical engineering sector had a profound effect on the economy and industry. Machine making, tool manufacture, steam-engine manufacture and general light manufacturing developed unprecedented levels of technical precision. The machine-making sector became a major employer, providing 167,000 jobs in 1870.

The mutual benefits of advances in iron and steel production and engineering are best illustrated in the progress of the growth of the shipbuilding industry. The relentless rise of the iron-clad steamship began in these years; it was to eclipse the traditional sailing vessel well before the end of the century. Growing overseas trade provided the market for the product, and, as technological innovation demonstrated the superiority of steam over sail, so production figures rose. The tonnage of new steamships averaged 12,000 tons per annum between 1840-49; but for 1870-79 this figure had reached 258,000 tons per annum. Cheap iron and steel made such vessels more competitively priced. Secondly, the development of more efficient marine steam engines provided a reliable and increasingly cost-effective form of power. In particular, the compound engine, developed by Clyde-based engineer John Elder, in 1854, allowed great fuel efficiencies to be made. This resulted in vessels requiring less coal for a voyage, allowing more space for cargo. The adoption of the modern propeller, known as the screw propeller, in the 1850s also improved fuel efficiency, being more economical than paddle propulsion.

The development of iron-clad steamships quickly transformed the geographical nature of the industry. The traditional wooden, sail shipbuilding industry, centred in the south and south west of the country was superseded by the new iron-steamship yards of the northern industrial regions, particularly on the Clyde around Glasgow, which produced 140,000 tons of shipping in 1874 alone. The Tyne, Tees, and Humber rivers also made rapid strides, sharing with Glasgow a proximity to the new materials of the shipbuilder, i.e. supplies of iron and steel and a developed skilled-engineering sector.

3 The Economic Impact of the Railways

The establishment of the railway network, outlined in the previous chapter, is fundamental to the prosperity of the mid-Victorian years. The full economic benefits of the system began to be felt once the largest cities and industrial regions had been linked, a process largely complete by the early 1850s. From this point, there existed a nation-wide network incorporating all the major conurbations, coalfields and ports of Britain, from the south coast, to the iron and coal region of South Wales, to the commercial and industrial Central Lowlands of Scotland. Rail travel had become an indispensable fact of economic life, and, whilst the impact upon personal travel had been more immediate, freight transport by rail added a new and powerful dimension to British industry.

The ability of the railways to serve the many branches of industry is illustrated by the following comment from the *Railway News*, describing the scene at principal London railway stations in 1864:

1   In the grey mists of morning, we see a large portion of the supply of the great London markets rapidly unloaded by these night trains; fish, flesh and food, Aylesbury butter and dairy fed pork, apples, cabbages and cucumbers and we know not what else, for the daily consumption
5   of London. No sooner do these disappear than at ten minutes interval arrive other trains with Manchester packs and bales, Liverpool cotton, American provisions. ... At a later hour of the morning, these are followed by other trains with the heaviest class of traffic - stones, bricks, iron girders and steel pipes.[10]

The mileage of track open between 1850 and 1875 increased from 6,084 to 14,500 miles, spreading the benefits of the railways and linking more businesses to the main trunk routes.

Any attempt to calculate the precise economic impact of the railways is difficult. There is no easy measure of the exact returns which accrued from them. What historians can do is isolate the general benefits of the system. The railway age, as the period is some-times referred to, fundamentally affected the course of economic development, and there are several reasons for this.

a) The Railways as a Source of Demand

One of the main beneficiaries of railway expansion was the iron and steel industry. By the end of the 1840s, up to 18 per cent of total iron production was committed to railway construction contracts. This included rail production, rolling stock, locomotives, signalling equip-ment and station construction. One result of this demand was the growth of specialist iron foundries producing rails, particularly in the developing South Wales iron industry. As steel became more readily and cheaply available with the adoption of the Bessemer Converter, so iron was gradually replaced as the preferred material for rail. Steel costs had fallen and although steel rails were still more expensive than iron (in 1862 one ton of steel rails cost £15 compared with £9 per ton for iron rails), the improved quality of steel ensured the greater durability of steel rails. Consequently, from the early 1860s, the steel industry received a considerable boost from railway contracts, whilst the iron industry continued to prosper from supplying a range of other products to the railway sector.

Coal consumption also increased with railway expansion, though this was not especially as a result of more coal being needed for steam locomotives; a source of demand accounting for only 2 per cent of total coal output. Of far greater significance was the need for more coal to fuel the iron and steel industry, as it strove to meet demand from the railway sector. A host of other industries which required more fuel to supply their product to the railways included bricks and glass.

Inevitably, the engineering industry benefited significantly. Precision engineering developed ever more powerful and reliable engines to satisfy the railway companies' demand for speed, comfort and reliability. Individual railway companies and specialist firms produced rolling stock and locomotives. Ultimately railway towns developed, such as Crewe, Swindon, Doncaster, Derby and Wolverton.

Employment directly associated with railway construction and operation boomed. Initially, the greater numbers were employed in construction, with at least 100,000 men being so occupied in the 1850s. The 1851 census identifies 65,000 people directly employed in the day to day operation of the network as drivers (4,000), porters (8,000), platelayers (4,500) and clerks (1,000), with the balance being made up from labourers and craftsmen in railway company work-shops. By 1873 such direct employment had risen to 275,000, with the larger companies such as the London and North Western alone employing 10,000 people, far greater than any individual manufac-turing company of the day. The 'multiplier effect' of this employment (whereby the wages paid to these workers created demand in the economy, leading to the employment of other workers, whose spending stimulated still further demand) was substantial, thus contributing to further general prosperity.

b) The Impact of Railway Transport on British Industry

Railways quickly demonstrated their value to the rapid transport of freight, particularly that of low-value, high-bulk products such as coal. Upon completion of the major trunk routes, the rapid expan-sion of freight movement by rail became a feature of British indus-trial development. In 1852, for the first time, the railway companies earned more from the transport of goods than from passengers. At the same time, the volume of goods moved by rail outweighed that conveyed by canal. Most of this traffic involved the conveyance of minerals. This is where rail conveyance demonstrated significant advantages in terms of cost, reliability and speed, although it must be noted that where speed of delivery was not a prime consideration, canals and indeed coastal transport remained important for the rest of the century. Nevertheless, by 1871, 65 per cent of mineral transport was by rail, of which 80 per cent was coal. Increasingly British industry became dependent upon the railway to meet its fuel transport requirements, and it was the rail network which helped overcome a potential bottleneck in fuel supplies which had threatened to overwhelm the overstretched canal network in the mid century.

The increased reliability of supply of raw materials, which the railways provided, had one further advantage. Companies could safely hold lower stocks of raw materials on their premises, thus freeing capital for more productive use. Furthermore, the railways may also have allowed greater flexibility of industrial location, particularly as a second phase of railway construction 'filled in the gaps' between the major trunk routes.

Access to markets, both domestic and overseas, was improved by better access to Britain's ports. A long-term benefit of the railways was the improvement in port facilities as port authorities competed for railway trade. Railway companies and port authorities developed new, more efficient facilities. In 1857, for example, the Northumberland Dock on the Tyne was constructed specifically to allow the delivery of coal by rail for dispatch by sea. Around the coast of Britain many ports improved their handling capabilities by developing their railway links. Some ports owed their very existence to the railway companies as they constructed their own ports, including Garston, near Liverpool, which opened for trade in 1853, Silloth (1859) and Grimsby (1852). Passenger ports such as Dover, Southampton and Holyhead also benefited from the provision of railway links.

The agricultural sector was quick to secure the benefits of rail transport, and through the improved supply of food, customers too benefited. Whilst the old drovers' trade deteriorated as a result of the movement of live animals by train, farmers secured higher profits on animals which arrived at markets heavier than they would have been under the old system. Perishable products, particularly milk, also arrived at market in prime condition. Indeed the railway network revolutionised the dairy trade in some areas as urban demand for fresh milk could be satisfied by farmers hitherto too remote from the major conurbations.

Business organisation too changed and modernised. The railway companies contributed greatly to the transformation of the structure of British firms, albeit over a longer timescale, as new managerial structures were introduced.

The creation of large-scale joint-stock companies with a hierarchical management structure was a feature of this period. This resulted from the development of ever larger companies through railway company amalgamations and take overs, especially in the 1850s and 1860s. Companies such as the London and North Western Railway, the Great Western Railway, or the Caledonian and North British Railway in effect created regional monopolies. Such companies developed management structures to deal with their increasingly complex operations. Boards of Directors were supported by middle managers who were often products of clear promotional routes within the company. Modern accounting procedures were introduced, with directors being accountable to shareholders for the company's profit performance. Hence the railways played more than a small part in the future development of joint-stock companies, providing a model for future organisational change across industry.

With the bulk of the railway network effectively complete by the 1870s, the full benefits of the network were being felt by the end of the mid-Victorian period. The most ambitious attempt to actually quantify the full impact of this railway expansion upon the British economy was made in the 1970s, by the economic historian G.R. Hawke. Hawke's statistical analysis of the performance of the railways for his chosen representative year, 1865, resulted in the most significant analysis to date of the true role of the railway in the British economy. Put simply, Hawke calculated the cost of transporting the same number of people and quantity of freight moved by rail by alternative available forms of transport in that year. Since the relative cost of rail transport was lower, the difference between the two calculations, i.e. between the actual total cost of rail transport in 1865 and the greater cost of the alternatives, represented what Hawke termed the social savings to society. The conclusion of his work suggested that, without the railways, national income would have been up to 11 per cent lower than it actually was.

Clearly, such statistical analysis is fraught with danger! Critics of Hawkes' work have pointed to the narrow statistical base upon which his work was calculated and of his reliance upon secondary sources. Nevertheless, the social-savings approach has proved to be a benchmark in attempting to assess the impact of the railways upon industry and the economy. It is clear that, without over-exaggerating the importance of the railways to the economy, they should be seen as a major contributory factor to the prosperity and unique economic experience of the years 1851-73.

4 Overseas Trade and the Economy

Whilst the home market remained the most important source of demand for British manufactured goods throughout the nineteenth century, foreign trade was always a major influence on the economy.

This was increasingly true of the mid-Victorian years. Imperial expansion, growing international wealth, in part due to gold discoveries abroad, and a desire among foreign states to emulate the British industrial experience are but three reasons why overseas trade expanded. It is the extent of the growth of international trade and its impact upon the British balance of payments which we must investigate first.

a) Trade Growth and the Balance of Payments

The growth in overseas trade reached unparalleled levels between 1850 and 1870. During this period the value of imports rose from £103 million to £303 million, whilst exports increased from £83 million to £244 million. At the same time total world trade had grown from an estimated £600 million to £2,700 million. Britain was by far the world's most important trading nation.

The principal British imports by 1870 included textile raw materials (which accounted for 27 per cent of totals in 1870), foodstuffs (34 per cent) and other raw materials (12 per cent). Manufactured goods accounted for just 3 per cent. These figures provide a number of interesting insights into the nature of the British economy. Clearly, the textile sector was strong; also we can see that the industrial sector satisfied, almost totally, the nation's demand for manufactures. On the debit side, the country clearly had difficulty providing sufficient foodstuffs to feed the growing population.

Export figures are similarly enlightening, lending support to the 'workshop of the world' thesis as Britain provided a range of products for the global market. In the same year, 1870, finished textiles accounted for 54 per cent of all exports by value, with cotton textiles alone providing 33 per cent. Although the total by value provided by textiles in 1850 had been 72 per cent, the lower figure 20 years later does not represent a decline in the volume of textiles sold. On the contrary, the volume of textiles sold abroad continued to increase. Rather, it represents the success of other exports in claiming a larger percentage share of the export trade. This was in fact good news for the economy, as Britain became less dependent upon one product. Other sectors which increased their export share include iron and steel (16 per cent in 1870), coal (4 per cent) and machinery exports (also 4 per cent). A broad range of products associated with the railway-engineering sector, including locomotives and rolling stock, became a major contributor to exports, with other manufactures such as glass and a range of domestic items also making a contribution. Finally, the re-export of colonial products initially imported into Britain makes up the balance.

It was, perhaps, the export of capital goods - machinery and other producer goods - which was most significant for the future. The confidence of British industrialists and governments in the nation's industrial lead allowed for the export of technology which foreign states might use to further their own industrial sectors and ultimately provide competition for Britain. Following the removal of restrictions on the export of machinery in 1843, British machine engineering had prospered from this increasingly lucrative export trade. Thus the industrialisation of France, Germany and the United States was aided to a significant degree by British technical expertise. Throughout the Empire, British technology was used to build railways and assist the exploitation of natural resources for export to Britain's industries.

An assessment of the overall importance of specific markets shows continental Europe accounting for an increased share of total British exports, from 30 per cent in 1850 to 40 per cent in 1870. The USA's share actually declined in the same period, from 26 to 18 per cent, although the total values of goods sold to the USA continued to increase. The smaller proportion of exports sold to the Americans is in part explained by difficulties encountered during the American Civil War and the erection of some tariff barriers by Washington in 1861 and 1864. As the relative importance of the American market declined, so new markets were exploited. China and, to a lesser extent, Japan proved increasingly lucrative. Colonial development, especially in the Indian sub-continent, Africa, Australia, New Zealand and Canada continued to provide growing markets for a range of British products.

If exports surged ahead, so too did the insatiable British demand for foreign produce. The import of foodstuffs, raw materials and luxury goods outstripped exports consistently in terms of value. An assessment of balance of payments figures demonstrates that, despite the growth of the economy, Britain remained in deficit with the rest of the world in terms of the 'visible' account, i.e. the trade in physical products. Yet this is not necessarily a negative comment on British economic performance. It can be viewed as a reflection of a buoyant economy, with industry needing increasing supplies of raw materials, many of which could only be obtained abroad. The increasing purchase of foreign foodstuffs reflects more than an apparent failure of British agriculture to feed the population. Such goods can, to a degree, be interpreted as a sign of rising domestic living standards as diets became more varied. Tea, coffee, sugar and some fruit and dairy products were increasingly seen as necessities. The growth in the import of luxury items - including wines and tobacco - is also a positive comment upon living standards. This is particularly true of the middle classes, the main beneficiaries of industrial prosperity.

Income from 'invisible' earnings, i.e. services such as shipping, insurance and banking, proved to be the factor which kept the overall balance of payments in credit. Net income from this sector trebled in the period, further enhancing Britain's role as the world's dominant trade and financial centre. To increasing numbers of British employers and workers, their personal prosperity was inextricably linked to Britain's role as the world's leading trading nation. To the supporters of free trade, this expansion was a complete vindication of their campaign to rid the country of trading restrictions.

British Balance of Payments, 1850-70 (Figures in £ million)		
	1850	1870
Imports	103.0	303.3
Exports	83.4	244.1
Net balance on visible account	-19.6	-59.2
Net invisible earnings	31.2	112.1
Balance of payments surplus	11.6	52.9

b) The Impact of Free Trade

In the light of growing prosperity, protagonists of free trade jubilantly proclaimed its success. The Victorian mind was, in fact, imbued by the early 1850s with the belief that the combination of prosperity and free trade was no coincidence. Indeed, the acceptance of free trade by both main political parties ensured that the days of protectionism were over. In 1849 the Navigation Laws were repealed. Since 1660, under the terms of these restrictive laws, imports into Britain and exports from Britain had been carried only on British ships or on ships of the country of origin of the imported product. In his two spells as Chancellor of the Exchequer (1852-55 and 1859-65) William Gladstone enthusiastically embraced the free-trade doctrine. In 1853, his budget reduced tariffs on a range of foods, including butter, eggs, cocoa and tea. In 1860, most remaining tariffs were removed completely, so that of the 1,146 items upon which duty was paid in 1840, only 48 remained in 1860. Most of these were upon luxury goods which did not figure in the lives of the majority. The Cobden-Chevalier Treaty between Britain and France, signed in 1860, provided for a major reduction in tariffs between the two nations and proved to be the last major act in the free-trade campaign until the end of the century.

The programme of trade liberalisation initiated by Peel in the 1840s, and brilliantly expounded by John Stuart Mill in his work *Principles of Political Economy* in 1848, was quickly followed by this unprecedented prosperity. The free-trade measures implemented by Gladstone and the growth of the 1850s and 1860s seemed simply to compound the link. Britons had looked forward to the benefits they felt free trade would inevitably bring, as a *Punch* cartoon of 1846 predicted. The British Lion might indeed comfortably enjoy the material benefits of cheaper food and luxuries from around the globe.

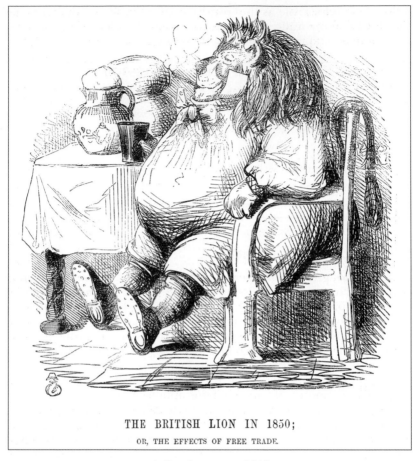

THE BRITISH LION IN 1850;

OR, THE EFFECTS OF FREE TRADE.

A *Punch* cartoon, 1846

However, the extent to which free trade was responsible for the apparent state of economic well-being is impossible to quantify. It is likely that Victorian advocates of free trade overestimated the impact the removal of tariffs actually had. Admittedly there were some benefits, and these are relatively easy to isolate. The psychological impact was probably significant insofar as the manufacturers and merchants felt free of interference in pursuing their various economic interests. The lower classes too had been persuaded of the inevitability of cheaper food and greater job security, particularly those employed in the export industries. Perhaps the most obvious tangible gain was on the diet of the masses: dairy products, tea, fruit, sugar and cocoa came increasingly within the financial reach of a greater number, particularly as real wage levels were showing modest signs of improvement. The opportunity to import grain free of tariffs from 1846 helped to ensure that the price of home-produced grain did not spiral upwards in response to growing demand as the population increased rapidly. Here was a cushion against the threat of higher prices in years of poor domestic harvests. A slow though steady growth of imported wheat resulted in 40 per cent of wheat consumed in Britain by 1870 being of foreign origin, compared to just 8 per cent in 1846. The actual price of wheat throughout the period showed little variation. The consequent benefit to industry was that the working classes, at a time of generally rising incomes, had more to spend on home-produced manufactures and less excuse to demand larger pay rises from employers.

On the other hand, there is less direct evidence to suggest that free trade was of great significance to industry. Industries relying upon imported raw materials arguably gained most, although Britain stood alone in its commitment to a liberalisation of international trade. In the USA, Prussia and France, infant industries were shielded from British competition by protective tariffs. Even the much vaunted Cobden-Chevalier treaty was signed for largely political rather than economic reasons, and the reality was that although tariffs overall between Britain and France were reduced the French retained tariffs of up to 30 per cent on British coal, machinery, iron and textiles. The role of free trade should therefore not be exaggerated. Of greater significance in explaining the growth in overseas trade is the growing demand from overseas for British products.

c) Britain and Overseas Demand

As the process of industrialisation in certain nations gathered pace, so Britain was well placed to exploit the opportunities this presented. After 1850 the push towards industrialisation in Europe and the USA created a demand for industrial products. The gold discoveries in California from 1849 and Australia in 1852 significantly increased the amount of money in circulation, providing the means to finance industrial expansion and, of course, to invest in railways. British industry found ready markets for a range of products from textiles to railways and ships to machinery of all types. In these developing

Steam-Engine Capacity in Europe and the USA, 1850-70 (Figures = '000 horsepower)		
	1850	1870
Germany	260	2,480
France	370	1,850
USA	1,680	5,590
Britain	1,290	4,040

industrial economies the latest technologies were employed, including the growing application of steam power being central to European and American industrial processes, as the table on page 81 shows.

It is conceivable that in the long term, by exporting such technology, British industry was contributing to its eventual demise as the world's foremost economic power. Hindsight supports this view; but for British companies at the time the opportunities presented were too lucrative to ignore, and of course such companies only dealt in the present or short-term future.

Overseas trade was also developing with many regions where there was little or no industrialisation taking place, such as in Africa or parts of the Far East. Thus, British firms traded with nations and regions of the world whose principal economic function for Britain was to supply raw materials and in return purchase manufactured goods. Colonial development is crucial in this regard as the extension of British imperial influence was inevitably tied in with the commercial exploitation of the colonies. The commonly-held assertion that 'trade follows the flag' can be something of a misrepresentation, as in many cases the reverse was true. Commercial gain was the primary motivation for much of Britain's imperial expansion in the second half of the nineteenth century.

Whatever the motive, the net result was that Britain increasingly dominated the world's trading network, controlling 40 per cent of international trade in 1873, while its highly lucrative 'invisibles' sector had established London as the world's premier financial centre. Overseas trade was thus one of the foundation stones of the mid-Victorian boom.

5 Finance and Banking

a) Joint-Stock Banking

The increasing complexity of both the domestic and international economy resulted in a major structural change in the banking sector in the middle decades of the century. The private, usually small-scale provincial banks (often referred to as the country banks), which had developed during the industrial revolution, were becoming increasingly inappropriate to the needs of a more sophisticated economy. Following legislation in 1826 and 1844, the greater liberalisation of banking allowed the expansion of banks operating under the joint-stock principle. Possessing greater reserves and being less vulnerable to localised, short-term crises, the joint-stock banks brought a greater degree of stability to the financial sector. To industry, the most significant contribution they made was a more flexible service by developing payment by cheque and easier means of transferring funds. Their role in providing investment funds was, however, less significant, as the principal source of funding for industry remained private investment or ploughing back profit into an existing business. Yet some banks did expand their role as a source of funding, especially for railway construction. Merchant banks continued to manage investment funds, though often dealing primarily with overseas investments.

In 1850 there were 99 joint-stock banks, with a total of 600 branches in England and Wales. By 1875, 122 such institutions possessed 1,364 branches and had eclipsed the old country banks in providing local banking needs. Emerging as leaders in this sector were Barclays, Midland, Lloyds, Martin and District banks, which became the premier high-street banks of the late nineteenth century.

b) Capital Funds and Capital Exports

Throughout the mid-Victorian period, the wealth of the nation increased substantially. Gold poured into London at a rate whereby the gold reserves of the nation increased six-fold between 1848 and 1855. A combination of increased British industrial prosperity and substantial earnings from overseas investments ensured that this trend continued. The net result was an increase in the amount of money in circulation and in the capital available for investment. Interest rates remained relatively low, averaging around 5 per cent over the period. Furthermore, the surplus of capital ensured that increasingly this money went into overseas investment opportunities. The growth of white, European settlement of the temperate areas of Australia, Canada, the USA and Argentina occurred, providing investment opportunities in mining and agriculture. Together these two activities accounted for 12 per cent of total British investment in these regions by 1870. Of far greater value was the 65 per cent of British overseas investment in railway construction and other infrastructure schemes such as dock construction. The great overseas investment booms occurred in 1855-60, 1862-66 and 1868-72. The total of such investments overseas, which stood at approximately £230 million in 1855, reached almost £1,000 million in 1870. In that year alone, interest on loans and dividends from shares realised a return to British investors of £44 million, accounting for over a third of 'invisible' earnings.

For industry therefore the mid-Victorian period was a time of opportunity and prosperity. For the country as a whole, the performance of the industrial sector was hugely beneficial, absorbing as it did a rapidly growing workforce. Employment prospects and income levels brought some improvement for the working classes, and for the middle class this period constituted a golden age. What may have surprised contemporaries more than anything was that, despite the advent of free trade, agriculture too shared in this prosperity.

6 Agriculture's 'Golden Age'

From the late 1840s to the early 1870s the agricultural sector succeeded in shaking off the problems of the post-Napoleonic depression and relative distress of the following quarter century. Instead, rural Britain experienced a prosperity which even the most optimistic of forecasters could not have expected. Modernisation was a key aspect of this prosperity. Agriculture embraced new technologies and science, disseminating knowledge more effectively and embarking upon land improvement schemes. It remains clear, however, that the 'Golden Age' was equally the result of factors outside the control of the agricultural industry itself. The inability of overseas producers to exploit British free trade is a major factor in understanding why British agriculture did not immediately face the ruinous effect of cheap grain, as predicted during the Corn Law repeal debates of the 1840s.

a) Free Trade and the Wheat Sector

The great fears over the potentially disastrous effects of repeal were not realised until the 1870s, when the extension of the railway into the North American heartland and the development of low-cost trans-Atlantic steamships brought a slump in grain prices in Britain. In the meantime, the delay allowed a period of prosperity in which wheat prices were, overall, maintained at pre-repeal levels.

Potential European sources of grain also failed to materialise in quantities which might have damaged the British agricultural sector as France and Russia found it sufficient challenge to feed the growing continental European population. The Crimean War of 1854-56 had

Wheat Prices, Average Per Annum for a Given Five-Year Period, 1830-74	
Year	Wheat price (shillings per quarter)
1830-34	57.67
1835-39	55.78
1840-44	57.85
1845-49	54.00
1850-54	49.03
1855-59	57.62
1860-64	49.78
1865-69	53.62
1870-74	55.00

further affected the situation, just as the American Civil War affected cotton textile production in the 1860s. For British farmers, a growing domestic population assisted the demand for home-produced grains and, consequently, there was no great retreat from wheat production and the acreage devoted to that crop was maintained.

b) Agricultural Improvement and 'High Farming'

Favourable prices and healthy market conditions encouraged Britain's farmers to seek improvements in the way the land was utilised. This affected more than the arable sector, with mixed husbandry (combining arable and pastoral farming) growing in popularity. The pastoral sector also experienced prosperity as demand for meat products increased. It was in the arable sector, however, where the most dramatic changes were felt. The importation of new fertilisers, most notably nitrates, in the form of guano from Peru and German potash, helped improve yields, especially when combined with improved drainage. In recognising the advantages of improved drainage, especially in the heavier clay soil areas, successive governments, from 1846, had made drainage loans available at the favourable interest rate of 3.5 per cent. The falling price of drainage pipes encouraged strong investment in such schemes, and total borrowing for this purpose reached £12 million by 1878. Better drainage made for easier and more effective ploughing, improving the return from fertilisers and allowing the greater use of mechanisation. Although machinery used on British farms was still limited to seed drills, threshing machines and improved ploughs, the economic climate encouraged a greater use of new techniques. Thus the arable industry enjoyed the twin benefits of higher yields and high demand. This extended beyond just wheat. Barley and oats experienced a 10 per cent rise in price over the period in response to growing demand.

Another feature of the 'Golden Age' was increased livestock production, often in combination with arable production. Mixed husbandry allowed farmers to react relatively quickly to price movements in either sector. In particular, many arable farmers were persuaded to develop the livestock side of their business, following increases in the prices of lamb, beef and dairy products.

The application of improved scientific knowledge in livestock breeding and the advent of rail transport for both live meat and fresh dairy products assisted the livestock farmer. In the more remote, often upland, pastoral regions, such as Scotland, Wales and northern England, a steady prosperity was experienced. Beef and mutton prices rose by 25 per cent over this period, though the product which experienced the most significant price leap was milk. Hitherto milk had been seen as a product carrying a high health risk. Growing incomes and easier access to fresh milk, courtesy of the railways, boosted demand for that product. Thus the technology of the railways came to the assistance of the agricultural sector.

Rising income levels across all social classes allowed the development of a more varied diet and the consumption of products previously the preserve of the better off. It is testament to the willingness and ability of the traditionally conservative agricultural sector that new practices and techniques were adopted. From 1846 to 1873, a total of £24 million was invested in the improvement of some 5 million acres. For landowners, the principal motivation was the ability to obtain higher rents from improved land. Tenant farmers supported such investment in the knowledge that favourable prices and increased yields would more than cover the higher rents.

However, the lessons of the post-Napoleonic war period had not been heeded by all. Doubt has been cast on the true value of the many improvement schemes. In draining thousands of acres of marginal land, many farms could not increase yields sufficiently to cover the cost of drainage loans. This was quickly apparent once prices fell in the mid 1870s. For those heavily committed to wheat, the fall in price was to prove catastrophic. Indeed for many small farms, of 100 acres or less, drainage schemes and investment in machinery could not produce sufficient rate of return to justify the initial outlay, and consequently improvements tended to affect the larger farms of 300 acres or more. Yet these constituted only a third of the farming community. Smaller farms also tended to be worked by farmers who were less informed and more conservative, preferring to retain traditional methods. They were thus less likely to be aware of the new ideas emanating from the much vaunted sources of agricultural research. Centres of excellence, like The Royal Agricultural Society, founded in 1838, Rothamsted Agricultural Research Station, and Cirencester Agricultural College, founded in 1843 and 1845 respectively, had little impact upon the working practices of most farmers.

As a result of the above, the inability of British agriculture, most notably the arable sector, to resist the challenge of overseas competition was quickly exposed. The 'Golden Age' of agriculture, and the high levels of production synonymous with 'High Farming', is best explained by the absence of serious foreign competition and favourable markets as the population grew and living standards improved rather than by a transformation in the quality of British agriculture. Advances were certainly made and this was undoubtedly a period of agricultural prosperity. But the depth of the subsequent depression in the arable sector has perhaps helped cast a more positive light on the achievements of the 'Golden Age' than might otherwise have been the case.

7 Conclusion

As we have seen, there is strong statistical evidence to support the view that this was a period of unprecedented growth and prosperity. We

Principal Forms of Occupation by Size of Workforce in 1871 (To nearest thousand)	
Agriculture	1,436,000
Domestic service	1,237,000
Labourer (general)	516,000
Cotton manufacture	482,000
Coal miner	371,000
Building trades	345,000
Milliner/dressmaker	301,000
Boot/shoe maker	223,000
Wool manufacture	220,000
Iron manufacture	180,000

must guard against any exaggerated view, however, that the transformation of the economy had even then transformed society. The 1871 census demonstrates that there still existed a strong traditional sector of the economy.

The figures quoted above reflect the findings of the official census of 1871. Unfortunately, they cannot be effectively compared with those for the census of 1851 since the methods of compiling totals had changed. The figures quoted here represent a more exact recording of specific types of employment. For example, the number of cotton and wool workers appears to have declined by 1871, compared to the 1851 census. This was, of course, not the case. The 1871 figures represent only those directly employed in the manufacturing process, whereas the 1851 figures represent all workers in the industry, including those involved in dyeing and processing.

Yet it is possible to determine the main, general trends in the economy, not least the fortunes of the agricultural sector, and here the contribution of agriculture to the economy fell over the period 1851 to 1871 from 21 per cent of national income to just 14 per cent. Despite the growth of the manufacturing sector, its contribution remained relatively static at 32 per cent. This is a reflection of the growth of other sectors, particularly transport, commerce, service industries and domestic service, all of which grew as a result of the increasing success and complexity of a modern economy.

It is, however, appropriate to conclude this section with a note of caution. Any economic analysis of the progress of industrialisation inevitably lacks a social perspective. A fuller appreciation of this period can only be achieved if one is aware that the rewards of economic success are rarely shared equally. In fact, severe poverty amongst the old, the infirm and the unskilled was very much a feature of British life. Annual average death rates in British industrial cities had remained almost unchanged between 1850 and 1875, at approximately 27 per 1,000 of the population. Of greater concern was the infant mortality rate which meant that, in the working-class quarters of such cities, 25 per cent of infants died before reaching their first birthday, despite the fact that in the period 1846-75, 29 sanitary acts had been passed. The working week for hundreds of thousands of workers still exceeded 60 hours and the great majority of workers, probably as high as 90 per cent, had no trades union to represent their interests. The pioneering work of many social investigators, such as Henry Mayhew, in the 1850s, demonstrated clearly the inequalities existing in British society. The idea of prosperity remained little more than a matter of statistics to a sizeable proportion of the population. Unemployment was an ever present threat for the unskilled and, as the 'Cotton Famine' had demonstrated, even those employed in the apparently successful sectors of the industrial economy were not immune to short-term economic downturns. This was apparent during the short, though severe, recession of 1858, when historians estimate that national unemployment reached 12 per cent, and despite recovering to just 3 per cent by 1865, the figures rose to 8 per cent in 1868.

Nevertheless, we must conclude that the economic rewards for the nation were great and the benefits of being first to industrialise allowed Britain to exploit international trade opportunities. This was just as well, as the following decades witnessed a serious challenge to the supremacy which made the mid-Victorian years unique.

References

1   R.A. Church, *The Great Victorian Boom* (Macmillan, 1975).

2   E.J. Hobsbawm, *The Age of Capital* (Cardinal, 1988), p. 44.

3   P. Mathias, *The First Industrial Nation* (Methuen, 1969), p. 251.

4   Ibid. p. 252.

5   R.C. Floud & D. McCloskey, *The Economic History of Britain Since 1700*, Vol. II (Cambridge, 1981).

6   E.J. Evans, *The Forging of the Modern State* (Longman, 1983), p. 276.

7   *Morning Chronicle*, 22nd October 1849.

8   *Chambers Edinburgh Journal*, 1858.

9   D.A. Farnie, *The English Cotton Industry and the World Market* (Clarendon Press, 1979), p. 96.

10 G.R. Hawke, *Railways and Economic Growth in England and Wales, 1840-1970* (Oxford University Press, 1970), p. 59.

Answering essay questions on 'The Zenith of British Economic Power'

Consider the following questions:
1. To what extent could Britain be regarded as an industrialised country by 1851?
2. 'Continuing growth and economic maturity are the major characteristics of the mid-Victorian period. Nevertheless, they did not lead to most of the population enjoying material comfort and security.' Discuss this assessment of the period 1850-73.
3. To what extent were the export industries the source of increasing prosperity between 1850 and 1873?
4. Assess the contribution of the railways to economic change between 1830 and 1870.
5. Analyse the main developments in British agriculture between the end of the Napoleonic wars (1815) and the onset of the 'Great Depression' (1873).

By the mid-Victorian period the economic transformation of Britain was well under way. The picture is one of social and political stability and, with the odd glitch, steady long-term economic growth. As there is also general agreement that 1850-73 was a period of prosperity, more emphasis is placed on explaining the general features and causes of this prosperity. The social history of the period rightly highlights the inequalities in the distribution of wealth, and students would be well advised to keep economic growth in perspective when writing on the economic success of the period. The above essays, then, reflect these points.

Question 1 develops the issue of industry and labour. This question will, of course, require you to use much of the material in Chapter 3 as well as Section 1 of this chapter. Much is made of the 'Workshop of the World' claims of contemporaries, indicating Britain's industrial supremacy. This is a question of perspective. The date of 1851 is a real aid to answering this question. Does the 'Great Exhibition' of that year support the claim that Britain was an industrialised society? 1851 was the year of the first truly modern and accurate census. What does that census tell us of the occupational structure of the population? How important were non-industrial occupations? You should also consider the relative sources of national wealth and how they were changing. Question 2 might be summarised as a 'yes, but' sort of answer! Illustrate the growth and explain the economic maturity; but you will need to demonstrate an awareness of the realities of life for the masses. Remember that the 'majority of the population' also includes the rural working classes as well as the more familiar urban population.

The relative importance of specific economic sectors is explored further in questions 3 and 4. Question 4 remains a popular question, though examiners are usually faced with a list of positive achievements of the railways. Can you demonstrate a more sophisticated understanding of the transport economics involved, as outlined in Hawke's 'Social Savings' theory mentioned in this chapter? Just how important were the railways? Has their role been exaggerated? What is the importance of the word 'change' in this title?

Finally, question 5 calls for an appreciation of the changing fortunes of agriculture over time. The causes of stagnation from 1815 to the 1840s, followed by the causes of relative prosperity, provide a clear structure. Introductions and conclusions are especially important here, allowing you to demonstrate your awareness of change over time. You might introduce your answer by highlighting the point of changing fortunes and conclude with the argument that the golden age was about to come to an end as the economy as a whole, and grain farmers, in particular, felt the chill wind of competition.

Source-based questions on 'The Zenith of British Economic Power'

1. An Alternative View of the Great Exhibition
Study the visual source entitled 'Specimens From Mr. Punch's Industrial Exhibition of 1850' on page 65.
a) Who is the taller of the two figures occupying the centre of the cartoon? Why is he included here? (4 marks)
b) What is the purpose of the cartoon? (6 marks)
c) Explain what each of the four 'exhibits' is intended to represent. (8 marks)
d) How is the exhibition to be 'improved in 1851'? (2 marks)

Hints and advice
Visual sources come in many forms, ranging from photographs to paintings and cartoons. The cartoon was a popular way of making, often satirical, political and social comment from the eighteenth century onwards. In particular, *Punch* magazine has proven to be a fertile source of visual evidence for historians of the nineteenth century. Invariably, such cartoons contain more evidence than might initially meet the eye, and you should take care to extract the maximum information and opinion from such examples. You should therefore take time to note all that you see. The cartoonist will only include material that he/she considers essential to the message. Try to draw out both the obvious and subtler messages contained in the source. They can be an invaluable guide to contemporary opinion and debate.

So, how do you set about answering (a)? Look at the way the figure is represented. Is he represented in a way that implies contempt or respect? Does he appear to be a figure of importance, even authority? How does he seem to view the 'exhibits' around him? What might be his link to the Great Exhibition of 1851? Do you recognise him from other illustrations? There is much more to explain for (b) as the marks available would suggest. This is clearly a question asking you to establish the motivation of the cartoonist. What are his concerns?

How does he portray the state of the 'exhibits'? Is he sympathetic or hostile towards them? Do his concerns go beyond the individuals shown? What, in your view, is the wider purpose of the cartoon?

In (c), you might focus more explicitly on the exhibits themselves. Why were these occupations chosen? How typical were they of the working classes generally? Why is the labourer's age specified and the shoemaker described as 'distressed'? Are they likely to be exhibits in the 'improved' exhibition of 1851? Why? Finally, (d) requires an assessment of the purpose behind the Great Exhibition of 1851. How would it portray Britain and British industry? How would it differ from the exhibition in the cartoon? Which presented the more accurate picture of Britain?

Summary Diagram
The Zenith of British Economic Power, 1851-73

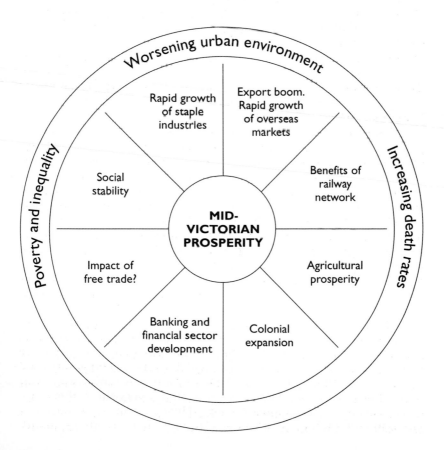

5 The End of Supremacy, 1873-1914

1 An Age of Controversy

Writing in 1934, the economic historian H.L. Beales suggested that 'there is something enigmatic about the "great depression" of 1873-96. It pervades all our textbooks with all the assurance of an established generalisation, yet in the lecture room its historical reality is greatly scouted [mocked]'.[1] By referring to a great depression in 1873-96, we immediately see that historians have singled out these years as worthy of specific attention. We see also that, as early as 1934, historians have debated the validity of the label 'great depression'. The word depression, when applied to an economy, might involve a slump in growth and sales, high unemployment, declining investment and a high rate of business failure. Yet today's accepted wisdom is that there was no such depression in these years. Although, as we shall see, the idea of depression may have seemed real enough to contemporary businessmen, it has been branded a myth by historians. General agreement exists that there was indeed a slowing down in the rate of growth of the economy, after the prosperity of the previous 25 years, but that no general depression existed. This leaves us with three fundamental questions to address in this chapter. Firstly, why did the term 'great depression' become such an entrenched feature of the language of the economic history of the late nineteenth century? Secondly, if historians have exploded the myth of the 'great depression', how effectively did the economy and industry perform during these years and how do historians explain that performance? Finally, should we therefore resist any temptation to view 1873-1914 as two distinct periods (1873-96 and 1897-1914)? An examination of the years from 1873 to 1914 as a whole will suggest that, in fact, this was a period of significant overall growth and that any such division is artificial and therefore inappropriate.

a) Contemporaries and the 'Great Depression'

Just as other labels attached to periods of British economic history (such as the 'industrial revolution', 'hungry Forties' and 'mid-Victorian prosperity') have come under scrutiny, so the 'great depression' of 1873-96 has been the subject of intense debate. The very term suggests images of falling production and exports, large-scale business failures, falling investment levels and high unemployment. Yet none of these was a general feature of the 1873-96 period. The phrase itself has contemporary origins. In 1878 the economist A.J. Wilson wrote in his work *Resources of Modern Countries* that 'everywhere there was stagnation and a negation of hope'. He complained of the poor condition of business enterprise, claiming that month by month

English exports were declining, and month by month producers were content to take lower prices. This apocryphal scenario was taken up by the Tory politician Randolph Churchill when, in 1884, he spoke of an economy suffering from a mortal disease. Why then were some influential and informed contemporaries moved to view the situation with such abject pessimism?

The first alarm bells had rung in 1873, when the volume of British exports actually fell. Nine years earlier there had been a brief fall in export figures, although this decline was reversed almost immediately. From 1873, however, the decline in export volumes was to continue to 1877. The result was a surge in the visible trade deficit from £60 million to £142 million. By 1885, despite some recovery in export volumes, Parliament appointed the Royal Commission on the Depression of Industry and Trade to 'inquire and report upon the extent, nature, and probable cause of the depression now or recently prevailing in various branches of trade and industry, and whether it can be alleviated by legislative or other measures.' The Commission reported the following year, providing what it described as a candid and accurate picture of the principal problems facing the economy. Its main findings, which were less alarming than contemporary business opinion may have expected, were:

i)   declining prices for agricultural products since 1873;
ii) an increased production of nearly all other classes of commodities;
iii) a tendency for the supply of commodities to outrun demand;
iv) a consequent diminution in the profit obtainable by production;
v)   a similar diminution in the rate of interest on invested capital.

The report noted furthermore that, although the unemployment situation as it stood in 1886 was cause for some concern, 'the general condition of the country affords encouragement for the future'. This was not a view universally accepted in the business world. The serious decline in industry's profits as a result of the factors noted above was of great concern to manufacturers, even if production and total sales were holding up. What then were the factors causing the decline in profits?

b) Prices and Profits

The years 1873 to 1896 saw a decline in actual levels of business profits. The crucial determining factor here is that of prices. The generally steady price rise of 1850-70 and the price surge of 1871-73 had brought with them unprecedented levels of profit. The subsequent price falls of 1873-96 inevitably impacted on profit levels also. The most eminent economist of the 1880s, Alfred Marshall, reported to another parliamentary commission in 1888 that price falls had created a severe depression in profits. The most dramatic falls occurred from 1873 to 1887 and, following a short-lived levelling out from 1888 to 1890, prices then fell a further 10 per cent in the years to 1896. Best estimates suggest an overall decline in wholesale prices of around 30 per cent for the whole period.

The causes of these price falls are complex and still the subject of disagreement amongst historians. Traditionally, they include the over-production of goods in the world market as a result of industrialisation elsewhere and the continued growth of the British industrial sector. The supply of goods was increasing at a faster rate than demand, pushing down prices. Secondly, the rapid development of improved industrial techniques and lower raw-material prices reduced costs of production. At the same time, transport costs were tumbling with the continued expansion of the world's railways and steam shipping. A more complex explanation exists which suggests that the growth of world production levels outstripped world gold production, as new gold discoveries declined. As more economies tied the amount of money in circulation to the gold reserves they held, so insufficient new money was generated to pay for the increasing stock of industrial goods and raw materials available, thereby depressing prices. The final explanation of falling prices involves an element of some or all of the above and perhaps others. What is clear is that the falling away of profit levels is to a large degree explained by this price fall. It is interesting to note, however, that profit levels rather than wage levels absorbed the greater impact. Employers chose not to lower wages to maintain profits. As a result, real wages increased substantially for the working classes (see pages 106-7). This may have been due to the need to compete for operatives as production continued to rise. To many contemporaries, the prime cause of the fall in profit which gave rise to the sense of depression was that of overseas competition.

c) The Threat of Overseas Competition

The industrialisation of European states such as Belgium, France and in particular the newly unified German state directly challenged British industrial supremacy in European markets from the 1870s onwards. Products such as textiles and iron and steel were hardest hit. At the same time the emerging industrial power of the United States affected British sales in North American markets. The expansion of tariff reform in both Europe and the United States to protect domestic industries, begun in the 1860s and extended throughout the latter decades of the century, reduced the competitiveness of British products. Some items, such as steel, incurred tariffs of 40 per cent. The absence of tariffs on imports into Britain led to calls for retaliatory measures from some quarters, although such voices were in the minority. The main concern was that, whilst British industry was effectively denied access to some markets, Germany and the United States were free to 'dump' their tariff-free products on the

British market. A series of contemporary pamphlets and articles presented the case of the Fair Trade League, established in 1881 in the light of this 'unfair' competition. Firstly, Edward Sullivan writing in 1881, in his article 'Isolated Free Trade', claimed that:

1 Now France and America and Belgium have got machinery, our machinery ... and our capital, and they are sending us a yearly increasing surplus that is driving our own goods out of our own markets; and every year they are more completely closing their markets to our goods. ...
5 When they see industries dying out under Free Trade in England, and springing to vigorous life under protection in France, Belgium, Germany and America, when they see the ruin of agriculture, the depression of all manufacturing industries ... capitalists preferring investments in foreign countries to those in their own ... they do not look much further for
10 arguments against Free Trade.

His fellow tariff reformer, W. Farrer Ecroyd, wrote in his pamphlet *Fair Trade* in the same year:

1 Our manufactures are more and more excluded from the markets of the civilised world, not by fair competition, but by oppressive tariffs. At home they are met by the unrestricted competition of every article which can be made more cheaply in any country by dint of longer hours
5 of work, lower wages. ... They enjoy the one advantage of cheap food, it is true; but that is purchased ... by the ruin of those dependent upon agriculture ...
   Under these circumstances it has been proposed to establish an import duty of 10 per cent on all foreign manufactures, not for protec-
10 tion, but to regain our power of bargaining with other nations, whose manufactures we buy, to admit ours as freely and fairly as we wish to admit theirs.

More extreme opinion emerged as, by the 1890s, Germany in particular became a target of the more xenophobic observers of Britain's relative decline. E.E. Williams, in a pamphlet entitled *Made in Germany* (1896), exemplifies the alarmist tone of some commentators:

1 Take observations in your surroundings. ... You will find that the material of some of your clothes was woven in Germany. ... The toys and the dolls made in German. ... Descend to your domestic depths, and you shall find your very drain pipes German made. ...
5 Roam the house over, and the fateful mark will greet you at every turn ... 'Manufactured in Germany'.

Even in the absence of those factors more usually associated with the concept of a great depression, it remains the case that contemporary business pessimism prevailed. Businessmen certainly thought that they were in a depression. More recently, however, historians have concentrated less on the terminology and more on the actual performance of the economy. As a result, they have uncovered a good deal of evidence which suggests that there were indeed some serious underlying problems which were to restrict future economic progress.

2 The Entrepreneur and the Relative Decline of Industry

A range of economic indicators confirm that British industrial growth was considerably slower than that of its main competitors in the last quarter of the nineteenth century. The end of the American Civil War and the economic emergence of what was soon to become Germany had not produced changes of such magnitude that British business felt threatened until the early 1870s. By the mid 1870s, however, the threat was increasingly apparent. Over the next 25 years, the loss of British supremacy continued relentlessly. But, it is important to realise that a loss of supremacy does not mean an actual decline in British industry. The economy continued to grow, though at a slower rate than in the previous two decades. Industrial production continued to increase, as did the volume of exports during the 1880s and 1890s. The key questions are, why did the rate of growth slow down and to what extent were Britain's competitors able to perform more effectively ?

Most significantly, the annual average rate at which the British economy grew over this period showed a marked decline. The figures are more dramatic when seen alongside those for the United States and Germany.

Relative Growth Rates: Britain, the United States and Germany Annual Average, 1873-1913			
	Total output	Industrial production	Output per worker
Britain	1.8%	2.0%	0.9%
United States	4.5%	4.7%	1.8%
Germany	2.8%	4.1%	1.4%

For Britain, the growth rates in the crucial export sector, the bedrock of mid-Victorian expansion, also slowed from an average of just under 5 per cent per annum between 1850 and 1870 to just 2 per cent per annum in 1870-90.

In 1870, Britain had accounted for a massive 31.8 per cent of total world manufacturing output, compared with only 22.3 per cent for the United States. Yet in 1913 the figures were 14.1 and 35.3 per cent respectively. In terms of value of exports, however, Britain still remained the world's most significant contributor by the end of the century.

Comparative Export Values (£ Sterling) 1870-99 (Annual averages per five-year period)			
	Britain	**Germany**	**France**	**USA**
1870-74	235	114	135	96
1875-79	202	132	138	125
1880-84	234	153	138	165
1885-89	226	151	132	146
1890-94	234	153	137	185
1895-99	238	181	144	213

Such figures demonstrate that in terms of goods traded in international markets, Britain was still in a predominant position. However, closer consideration tells us that her competitors were expanding their exports at a faster rate. Furthermore, American industry was able to satisfy demand in a domestic market far larger than that of Britain, whilst still exploiting new export markets. Germany and France were making inroads into European markets at Britain's expense, whilst British manufacturers were forced to rely ever more heavily on the Empire market. Indeed the possession of an empire which naturally leaned towards British goods distorts the picture, although even here the USA had by the end of the century comprehensively overtaken Britain in exports to Canada. What, then, are the explanations for this relative retardation in British industrial performance?

a) Complacency and Conservatism

A strongly critical view of the British entrepreneur, popularised by the historian D.S. Landes in the 1960s, takes the view that the British entrepreneur of the late-nineteenth century lacked the innovative and enterprising zeal of his predecessors. The current leaders of the family firms which dominated British industry held the position of manufacturer, industrialist or merchant as a birthright or inheritance rather than as a reflection of business acumen. This interpretation assumes that the new generation of industrialists was neither interested in the firm other than as a source of continued profit for the family nor particularly well-equipped in a business sense to take Britain into a more competitive world.

In many firms, claimed Landes:

1   the grandfather who started the business and built it by unremitting application and by thrift bordering on miserliness had long died; the father who took over a solid enterprise and, starting with larger ambitions, raised it to undreamed of heights, had passed on the reins;
5   now it was the turn of the third generation, the children of affluence,

tired of the tedium of trade and flushed with the bucolic aspirations of the country gentleman.[2]

Historians have isolated a number of factors which suggest that some British entrepreneurs did lack the competitive edge of their foreign competitors. The inherent conservatism of many British industrialists is a central feature of this question of entrepreneurial performance. S.B. Saul develops this sociological theme in comparing British and American attitudes towards trade and industry. The class system, it is suggested, ensured that men of industry enjoyed considerably less prestige in Britain, where family, education and accent were a more reliable passport to acceptance in higher social circles. This was far less an issue in the United States, where achievement was more readily measured through success in business and personal wealth. The power, prestige and influence held by men such as the American steel magnate Andrew Carnegie bear testimony to this.

Whilst there may be some evidence to support this view, we return to the issue of conservatism in business rather than in society at large to get to the heart of British entrepreneurial failings. Here it is important to distinguish between entrepreneur and manager. The problem was more pronounced in those family firms which lacked the specialist, professional managers, who were far more common in German or American companies. The owners of such British firms were often reluctant to experiment in new products, invest in new techniques or develop new markets so long as profits continued. Although profits may have been lower, the income drawn from that profit was the key to social standing and thus the maintenance of a lifestyle. As a result, reinvestment of ploughed-back profit reduced during this time of lower profits. A closer look at British business and the entrepreneur provides clear examples of such failure.

b) Business Structures

One of the most striking differences between the structure and organisation of British companies and their German or American counterparts was that of size. In key industrial sectors such as steel and coal, both Germany and the United States witnessed the rise of huge companies which dominated whole sectors. A favoured trend in both countries was the creation of combinations of companies which might merge into one very powerful corporation or simply operate as an association known as a cartel, controlling production and prices within an industry. The adoption of 'horizontal integration' was therefore common: companies operating at the same stage of the production process (e.g. steel mills) would join forces. This process often developed further, resulting in 'vertical integration', whereby companies would merge with, or take over, other firms involved in different levels of the production process. (Thus, to illustrate vertical integration, a steel producer might integrate with firms mining iron ore for their steel mill, or with the heavy engineering companies which turned the steel into steel girders or rails.) These actions created industrial concerns far bigger than their British rivals. In Germany, the great Krupps steel firm was a central influence in an association which consisted of 30 steel mills by 1911. In the United States similar great corporate institutions developed. For example, the domination of the American steel industry made Andrew Carnegie one of the world's richest men. A further example is John D. Rockerfeller, who created and controlled Standard Oil.

The huge wealth and power of such individuals and corporations was not matched in Britain, whose businessmen had been raised on the principles of *laissez-faire* economics and free and open competition, and in consequence where integration, cartels and limited liability companies were exceptions. Price-fixing was on a far smaller scale in Britain. Such actions were considered, rightly, not to be in the public interest. On the whole, British industry adhered to the maxim of competition, a policy which in the minds of British entrepreneurs was central to the wealth and influence which the nation enjoyed.

Part of the problem in Britain was the continued predominance of the small firm. As late as 1914, only 23 per cent of British companies were not privately owned as family firms or partnerships. In the British coal industry, for instance, just under 1,600 companies owned the nation's 3,300 pits in 1913. In the German Ruhr coal region, in sharp contrast, total production was controlled by no more than 12 companies. A similar pattern existed across the manufacturing sector. The implications for British competitiveness were significant. Larger corporations held a number of advantages including the build-up of significant capital reserves which offered better protection against market fluctuations. Such firms were better placed to invest in new technology, and in higher quality research and development, and so they attracted the most able professional managers and technicians. It is no surprise therefore that the most significant technological developments of the late nineteenth century, including electrical engineering, the internal combustion engine, improved dye-stuffs and chemicals, and even typewriters and sewing machines, emanated from Germany and the United States rather than Britain.

As mass production developed, pioneered in the United States, so standardised measurements, parts and products became more common. In Britain, on the other hand, there were - with a few exceptions - too many small companies producing unique, individually crafted, products which took longer to produce, were more expensive and had little standardisation across the sector.

c) Over-Commitment to the Staple Industries

The failure to fully develop the potential of the 'new' technologies and industries resulted in the continued dependence of the country on the same industries which had brought prosperity in the mid-Victorian years. This over-commitment to older export sectors, and to their long-established markets, is seen as a manifestation of the entrepreneurial conservatism and structural weaknesses which were to prove so damaging to the long-term future of the economy. The continuation of investment in these industries disguised fundamental inefficiencies. Part of the problem, ironically, was that textiles, coal, engineering and iron and steel continued to make profits. Production levels continued to grow and markets overseas could still be found in the 1890s and 1890s. Entrepreneurs opted for a cautious approach to investment, given their pessimistic concern over falling profit levels. Tried and tested technology remained in force in cotton textiles, where larger spinning mills still used the old techniques of mule spinning when competitors had shifted to the more advanced technology of ring spinning. In the coal industry, the adoption of coal-cutting machinery was relatively undeveloped. It is only partly explained by the size and geological complexity of British coal seams compared with those in the USA, where by 1900, 20 per cent of coal was extracted by the new technology. In Britain the figure was less than 2 per cent. The relatively high cost of labour in the United States had encouraged such a development, whereas in Britain coalminers were cheap and plentiful. In 1873, 465,000 miners had worked Britain's coal pits; in 1900 the figure was 820,000.

The experience of the steel industry too suggests a reluctance to exploit new opportunities. A radical technological breakthrough had occurred in 1879 with the discovery of a technique known as the Gilchrist-Thomas or Basic Process, which allowed iron ore containing phosphorous to be used in the production of cheap steel. Most British, American and German reserves were phosphoric. Yet whereas her competitors quickly embraced the new (ironically British!) discovery, British steel masters have been accused of dragging their feet, wringing out the last profits from the Bessemer Converters in which Britain had invested heavily.

The American industrialist Andrew Carnegie made the point in the 1890s that most British equipment was in use 20 years after it should have been scrapped. It was, he claimed, because Britain kept this used-up machinery that America increasingly out-performed Britain.

This conservatism stifled the development of a modern industrial base. As investment continued in the 'safe' staple industries, so the economy relied on them to provide work, exports and wealth. In 1900 half of British industrial production and 70 per cent of her exports came from the same industries which had been the cornerstones of the industrial revolution, 100 years before.

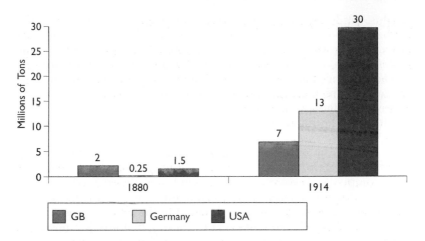

Steel Production in Britain, Germany and the USA between 1880 and 1914

d) Investment

The investment record of British entrepreneurs has also been cited as a cause of relative decline. Here the problem was twofold. The preference for 'safe' investment in existing technology has already been outlined, reflecting the conservatism of British industrialists. A second issue is that of the availability of investment funds, and here the picture is far less clear. It is a reasonable assumption that declining profit levels resulted in lower levels of ploughed-back profit. However, an area of debate still unresolved is the role of the capital markets, including banks, in making funds available for investment in domestic industry. S.B. Saul isolates the main issues of the debate:

> 1 It has been suggested that overseas investment deprived the home market of funds. ... An alternative argument is that the capital market was poorly geared towards the supply of funds for industry at home. ... The problem is to assess how far industrial growth was inhibited by
> 5 institutional difficulties of this kind and how far it is accurate to argue that money did not flow into business because industrialists did not wish to borrow. The small size of many companies and the tradition of self finance were serious hindrances.[3]

There is strong evidence to suggest that all the above explanations played a role in ensuring that the financial relationship between capital markets and industry was far less close in Britain than, for example, in the United States or Germany. In particular, the growth in capital exports would suggest a preference for foreign investments which yielded a higher return than investments at home. The growth of available investment funds throughout the so called 'great depression' years shows clearly that 'capital formation', i.e. the amount of surplus funds available for investment, was not a problem. This further supports the belief that there was no actual depression. Indeed the growth of overseas investment reached boom proportions after the turn of the century. By 1914 Britain was the dominant force in world finance and the world's major creditor, accounting for 41 per cent of total international investment. British overseas assets totalled a massive £4 billion at the outbreak of the First World War.

Whilst we cannot accurately assess the impact this had on domestic industrial investment, we might perhaps conclude that the pessimism which existed in British business circles hardly encouraged internal investment. At home the railway building programme had long been completed. However, in foreign markets, the investment opportunities in this area continued. In the United States, for instance, the total value of British investment doubled in the 1880s alone.

However, before condemning the money markets for neglecting the domestic economy, it is essential to remember that the British entrepreneur remained reluctant to fund investment through this source. Thus we return to the issue of the conservative traditions of British industry. In any case the money market of London had itself established a tradition of involvement in overseas investments, partly as a result of these long-established domestic investment patterns. Put simply, the British banking system was becoming more internationalist in its outlook. Inevitably and ironically therefore, British investment played a significant part in the funding of American and European industrialisation.

e) Technical Education and British Industry

In an increasingly technological age, the need to develop a more skilled, technically accomplished workforce is central to a competitive economy. The development of technical education in Germany was a significant factor in that nation's improving industrial performance, particularly in chemicals and various branches of engineering. Research and development in both Germany and the United States was considered an essential function of industry. As early as 1867, at the International Exhibition of that year, it was clear that Britain's hitherto slowly emerging competitors had made great technical advances since the Great Exhibition of 1851. The initial British response was the setting up of a House of Commons Committee to consider the issue of technical education in Britain. As a result of the continued boom in the late 1860s and early 1870s, however, no concrete action was taken and the negligible provision of technical education continued until the late 1880s. The resistance of British employers to providing opportunities for high-quality technical education was part of the unfortunate tradition of conservatism. The view that a skill was acquired on the shop floor rather than in the lecture room or the laboratory remained strong. Indeed the

British entrepreneur was renowned for his suspicion of the expert. The history of British industry in the late nineteenth century is consequently littered with examples of engineers who made poor businessmen and businessmen who lacked an advanced level of technical and scientific understanding, preferring the safety of tried and tested - though increasingly out-dated - technology. Since the State had only recently made the most elementary education compulsory and freely available to British children through three Acts of Parliament in 1870, 1876 and 1880, it is perhaps not surprising that technical education was not seen as a major priority. Although technical education did develop reasonably successfully from the 1890s, particularly amongst men in the engineering trades, Britain was already lagging behind her competitors in the 'new' industries such as motor manufacturing, electrical engineering and chemicals.

The slowness of British industry in switching to new techniques, such as electrical power in place of steam, had affected the perceived need for high levels of technical education. By 1914, Britain had only 9,000 university students, of whom only a minority studied technical or scientific subjects. Germany had seven times as many. It may be appropriate, therefore, to see this as a problem of government and society generally rather than simply of failings in the industrial sector. In the late nineteenth century, State aid for education was paltry. As the historian Michael Sanderson claims, 'The Englishman had yet to learn that an extended and systematic education, up to and including methods of original research, was now a necessary preliminary to the fullest development of industry.'[4]

The advent of technical qualifications, such as City and Guilds of the London Institute examinations from 1879 and the Technical Institutions Act of 1889, which allowed county councils to make available funds for establishing technical education, were both welcome developments; and in the future, technical education expanded rapidly. However, in the time taken to achieve this advance, the initiative had been surrendered to Britain's competitors in key industries. Undoubtedly, in the late nineteenth century, Britain possessed a number of brilliant individual engineers. What she lacked was the necessary ranks of trained technicians vital to the future.

3 Economic Performance in Perspective

The clearest manifestation of the underlying problems affecting British industrial performance is straightforward. She increasingly 'failed to produce and distribute an array of goods and services similar to that supplied by other industrial economies with an efficiency comparable to theirs.'[5] However, a contradiction exists in that, whatever the quality of entrepreneurial performance in the last quarter of the nineteenth century, it remains a paradoxical historical fact that the British economy experienced continued overall growth. It is in the context of growth that we must consider any shortcomings, as continued expansion of production, sales and exports inevitably influenced the decisions of the manufacturing sector regarding new investments. Without going too far in attempting to rescue the reputation of British entrepreneurs, we must nevertheless admit that, viewed from their perspective, conservatism in investment and business practice made sense in a time of what they considered to be depression. At least existing industries and technology made some profit, albeit lower than before, and production levels continued to rise.

Production Indicators (per decade) of the Staple Industries				
	Coal output (million tons)	Steel output (million tons)	Steam ships (Built and first registered in Britain '000 tons)	Cotton textiles (Raw-cotton imports million lbs)
1870-79	127	0.68	258.6	1,244
1880-89	160	2.3	377.2	1,473
1890-99	191	3.6	500.9	1,557

Such economic indicators, although offering a restricted insight into economic activity, support the assertion that this was not a period which fits the image of depression. A relative decline in British economic dominance did not mean absolute decline, and it is therefore important to judge Britain's performance in perspective.

a) Competitors and Comparisons

Whilst we should not underestimate the significance of growing overseas competition, there are clear dangers in applying direct comparisons of British industrial performance with that of her major competitors. Firstly, percentage growth rates of respective economies can present a distorted picture. Beginning from a smaller industrial base, a relatively small increase in output, when viewed as a percentage of total production, can seem very impressive. However, a growth rate of 10 per cent in an economy producing 100 units is in fact far less significant than an economy which manages a 5 per cent growth rate per 10,000 units produced. Consequently, we should not overstate the extent to which Britain seemed to be outperformed. For example, the German shipbuilding industry may have achieved higher growth rates than that of Britain in the 1880s and 1890s, but Britain remained the world's major producer of ships in the years before the First World War.

A distortion of the exact picture also occurs when comparing the performance of the world's best examples in specific industrial sectors. Quite simply, Britain could not expect to out-perform all nations in all areas of industry. Direct comparisons with German chemicals and American automobiles present an exaggeratedly negative picture. It is important to remember that the loss of supremacy was in fact inevitable once the economic and industrial potential of the United States and Germany, with their massive resources, was finally harnessed. As these nations embarked upon industrialisation, they could also benefit from the British experience. The possibilities for economic advancement, national and personal wealth and technical progress, so clearly seen in Britain, spurred nations on to adopt British technology; and from this initial industrialisation such nations were able to develop their own industrial and technological skills. Furthermore, each industrialising nation possessed specific advantages which encouraged rapid industrialisation. The United States, Belgium, France and Germany all possessed coal reserves essential to industrial progress. Germany and the United States also held huge reserves of accessible iron ore. All invested in the latest technologies, whilst British entrepreneurs remained committed to machinery and plant in which they had already invested heavily. Thus we have the irony of the latest textile technology from the world's most advanced firms, such as Platts of Oldham, being adopted around the world, whilst British firms - on the doorstep - worked with machines installed by previous generations.

The threat posed by the United States to Britain was particularly serious. The political stability of the post-Civil War period allowed the economic development of a huge country endowed with vast mineral reserves and agricultural potential. Her liberal immigration laws encouraged the rapid growth of the population, providing workforce and customers, both of which encouraged economic expansion. The prevailing optimism, and the belief that industrial and agricultural enterprise was open to all, was in stark contrast to the situation in Britain. In the United States direct government intervention, through the adoption of protective tariffs, provided a climate in which domestic industry could thrive. Seen in these terms, it is inevitable that Britain would be usurped by this emerging giant.

Whilst the Fair Trade League had proposed retaliatory tariffs, the generally held belief that free trade was still on balance good for Britain remained intact. There were good reasons for this. Firstly, free trade ensured low food prices. (As we shall see in the next section, this had major implications for certain sectors of British agriculture.) The newly enfranchised working man (following the reform acts of 1867 and 1884) would have viewed with concern any action which raised food prices. Low food prices also released more cash for the purchase of manufactured goods. Finally, low raw-material costs allowed by free trade were now especially important at a time of low profits.

In reality it would appear that the 'catching up' effect by competitor nations was natural and inevitable. Some historians have suggested that Britain's early start to industrialisation placed her at a disadvantage later, as competitors learned from her mistakes. However, the idea that somehow Britain was unnecessarily paying the price for being the first to industrialise has little to support it. A slower rate of growth was unavoidable in the circumstances, and although the slow down in the economy is in part due to entrepreneurial failures, it was not possible to resist or ignore the increasing industrialisation of the western world.

b) Price-Falls in Perspective

The general decline in prices, as of percentage growth rates, must also be considered with caution. The resulting fall in the profit gained from each unit produced does not automatically signal a decline in the economic health of the nation. We should first of all see price falls in the context of the price rises of the 1850s and 1860s and the short-term boom in prices at the start of the 1870s. Prices in 1878 were still on a par with the price levels of 1850. Thereafter the steep fall in prices (see the table below) brought with it some clear advantages. Certain commodities, such as coal, with its booming export trade, managed to sustain prices to a degree after the initially dramatic slump of 1873-75. The prices of animal products were also resilient (see page 111). Imported foodstuffs experienced the most rapid falls.

Cheaper products helped expand export sales. Of great significance to Britain was the shift of the terms of trade in her favour in the 1880s and 1890s: the fall in the price of imports was greater than that in the price of exports. As Britain imported 50 per cent of her foodstuffs by 1900, and a substantial proportion of industrial raw materials, the benefits become clear. The working-class family gained most. Prices fell but wage levels remained fairly constant. Therefore 'real wages' (wages in relation to prices) increased very significantly, with living standards rising more quickly than at any other time since industrialisation began. The general consensus is of an improvement of around

			Sugar, Tea,	
	Metals & coal	Grain	Animal products	Tobacco, Coffee & Cocoa
1871-75	100.0	100.0	100.0	100.0
1876-80	66.7	95.4	102.6	92.0
1881-85	60.7	83.7	98.6	83.5
1886-90	61.5	67.7	84.8	70.6
1890-95	63.6	66.0	84.6	68.3

Index of Relative Price Falls in Selective Commodities, over 5-Year Periods

25-30 per cent for the 1873-96 period. This overall rise in real incomes offset the losses experienced in the short-term rises in unemployment levels, such as 1879, 1885-87 and 1892-95, when unemployment peaked at 12 per cent. At other times the unemployment rate was low, though the average for the whole period was 7.2 per cent, compared to 5 per cent for the period 1850-70. (These figures are not considered absolutely accurate as no official records were kept until the early twentieth century.) However, given that the rise in population resulted in a 10 per cent per decade growth of the working population, hundreds of thousands of new jobs were being created.

c) Entrepreneurial Success

The psychological blow of lower profits and loss of supremacy should not eclipse the achievements of some sectors of the economy. Neither should generalised criticisms obscure the importance of individual cases of progress and technological advance. Whilst Britain undoubtedly lagged behind in some new industries, new sectors were created and established with some success. There was progress, beyond simply increasing production, in the staple industries. The much criticised steel sector did eventually break from its commitment to the Bessemer process. Teesside emerged as a centre of the steel sector, utilising the major phosphoric ore deposits of the Cleveland hills. Middlesborough became a steel-boom town, increasing its population from just 19,000 in 1861 to 91,000 by 1901. Lancashire cotton continued to increase exports and develop Far Eastern markets in response to its exclusion from other markets. By 1900, annual exports had risen to 5 million yards of finished cloth, from an average of 3.5 million in the 1870s. Coal exports had doubled, from 15 million tons per annum average in the late 1870s to almost 30 million tons by 1895.

For the longer term, the development of new sectors was vital, and here it is necessary to record the establishment of such industries. As steam had dominated industrial power in the nineteenth century, so electrical power and internal combustion were the key to the twentieth. Electrical engineering, especially power generation and supply, was gradually established, creating a rudimentary power grid by 1900. The development of an electrical light source, the incandescent lamp by Thomas Edison in the United States and by Joseph Swan in Britain, provided the opportunity for industrial, domestic and street lighting. The Steam Turbine, produced by Briton Charles Parsons, dramatically improved the efficiency of power stations from 1884, and in part allowed the extension of electrical power to transport (trams and railways), although the production of electrical appliances was dominated by Germany and the United States.

The British motor industry was always lagging behind that of the United States, France, Germany and Italy. Nevertheless, small-scale manufacturers proliferated in the years leading up to World War One. The repeal of the Red Flag Act in 1896 (before which time any mechanically powered vehicle was restricted to a maximum speed of 4mph and preceded by a pedestrian carrying a red flag!) belatedly gave the domestic industry a boost. The principal problem for the industry was, once again, the size of individual companies. Cars were individually produced, ignoring the more cost-efficient methods of mass production being pioneered abroad. It was also apparent that engineers and not businessmen ran companies. Indeed, in many respects the fledgling motor industry actually displayed most of the structural defects of British industrial organisation. As Dintenfass explains, this was a prime test of Britain's responsiveness to the techniques of mass production - a test of Britain's capacity to innovate in the absence of constraints imposed by an early start.[6] It would appear that she largely failed the test. Nevertheless, some manufacturers, with a reputation for quality if not affordability, not least Rolls-Royce, emerged in the pre-war years, from the 200 or so companies who had entered the motor industry. Few prevailed for very long and it was left to the likes of Ford of the United States to exploit the cheaper end of the market.

The motor car remained a luxury item, unavailable to the masses, and yet developments in the bicycle industry allowed something of a personal mobility revolution lower down the social scale. Britain became the major player in the development of a bicycle industry, concentrating production in the metalworking expertise of the Midlands. British Small Arms, Humber, Stanley and Raleigh contributed to an industry worth £2 million to the export trade by 1900.

There is no doubt that the choice and affordability of consumer products was increasing, and this gave rise to a mass market for such products in the late nineteenth century. Hence there was a corresponding growth in the service sector. The most obvious manifestation of a consumer boom was the rise of the retail 'multiples' in Britain, where one company owned many branches of its stores: these included some names well-known to today's consumers, including W.H. Smith, Lipton's, and Boots. Whilst their contribution was relatively small-scale to the economy as a whole, their growth marks the beginning of the new era of growing consumerism which was to dominate the twentieth-century economy.

4 The 'Agricultural Depression'

The dangers associated with the generalisations and exaggerated claims of depression in the industrial sector are replicated in the experiences of British agriculture between 1873 and 1896. However, there were in agriculture very real signs of severe difficulties in the arable sector. The still powerful though diminishing influence of the landed classes ensured that the problems of the land were loudly publicised. This culminated in two parliamentary Commissions investigating the industry. The findings of the Richmond Commission (1879-82) and the Royal Commission on Agriculture (1894-98) provided contemporaries with a picture of decline which deepened the sense of depression. By the late 1870s it seemed that the period of 'High Farming' was over. The Richmond Commission reported its views of the causes of the problem in 1882:

1   All the witnesses we have examined have agreed in ascribing it mainly to a succession of unfavourable seasons. One witness says: It is really owing to the absence of sun and the presence of an extra quantity of rain. ... Nothing in fact in the last two years has matured
5   properly. ... Next to unfavourable seasons as a cause of agricultural depression, foreign competition is alleged to have produced the most injurious effect. ... The unexpectedly large importations, chiefly from America, have, by lowering prices of home produce greatly increased agricultural depression. ... The effect of the Education Act has been
10 referred to by several employers of labour as seriously interfering with farm work. ... There prevails complete uniformity of conviction as to the great extent and intensity of the distress which has fallen on the agricultural community.

Sir James Caird, the most influential agricultural writer of the time, warned in 1878, in his work *The Landed Interest and the Supply of Food*, that the continued problems associated with the small farms (see page 86) posed a long-term threat to the future of agriculture. Added to this was the continued issue of short-term, sometimes annual, tenancies which, he claimed, deterred many farmers from switching from grain and investing in more profitable areas such as meat or dairy products. The longer leases generally issued in Scotland had, he felt, contributed to the healthier state of Scottish arable agriculture. Caird also felt that the industry was being left by a *laissez-faire* government to the forces of the free market.

That there was a crisis of declining arable prices is beyond doubt, as the table over leaf demonstrates.

The fundamental cause of the problem was, of course, foreign competition, despite the link established with poor weather by contemporaries. In the past, poor weather and bad harvests, by diminishing production, had raised prices; but this did not happen now, and with a renewal of good weather after 1882 prices fell further. As railways made inroads into the American prairies, the production of cheap grain there soared. Cheaper trans-Atlantic freight costs brought unprecedented quantities of low-cost wheat to Britain, free of tariffs. Imports doubled between 1875 and 1900, reducing wheat from 47 shillings (£2.35) per quarter, to 27 shillings (£1.35). This caused a 40 per cent cut in the average price of bread.

Index of Prices for English Arable Crops, 5-Year Annual Averages, 1870-1913 (1867-77=100)				
	Wheat	Oats	Barley	Potatoes
1870-74	101	97	99	98
1880-84	78	83	82	84
1890-94	54	73	68	63
1900-04	50	69	62	68
1910-13	59	74	69	69

a) The Impact of Depression in the Arable Sector

The results of such competition and price falls were wide-ranging. The main grain regions of the south, south-east and Lincolnshire bore the brunt of the arable depression. In such areas the principal victim was the agricultural labourer, as farmers sought to protect themselves by cutting wages and reducing the workforce. As a percentage of the total labour force, agriculture claimed just 9 per cent in 1900, compared with 20 per cent in 1851. The main loss of workers occurred in the 1870s when the sudden slump in prices occurred and farmers had little time to adjust. By 1881, the percentage of workers in agriculture had already fallen to 12.6 per cent of the total. A major exodus from the land between 1873 and 1882 saw 300,000 rural inhabitants leave for urban employment or emigration (especially to North America and Australasia). Inevitably, rural poverty also increased as agricultural wages fell and employment opportunities diminished. In East Anglia, weekly wages for labourers averaged 11s 6d (57.5p), which was roughly half that of the urban labourer. In the less depressed pastoral areas, agricultural wages were higher, at 16s 10d (84p) per week on average, though this still compares unfavourably with average industrial wages in 1881 of 28 shillings (£1.40). (It should be noted that these figures do not take into account the fact that many agricultural labourers were provided with accommodation by employers, thus reducing the difference in real wages between agricultural and industrial workers.)

Many farmers could not afford the cost of conversion to pastoral production, which would involve new buildings and the purchase of stock. Added to this was the fact that the cost of cultivating the marginal lands, which were only profitable when prices were high, proved not to be worthwhile, and so they were left fallow. Some farmers did make the belated switch to other crops or to pastoral grassland. The net result was a fall in acreages given over to grain. In 1870, 3.3 million acres were cultivated for wheat; and by 1910 this had fallen to 1.7 million. For barley the figures were 2.1 million down to 1.5 million for the same period. Permanent pasture land, however, rose from 11.1 million acres to 15.9 million. The value to landowners of such land also declined, with arable rents falling by some 25 per cent, in the process reducing investment in the land. This decline in investment had longer-term implications for the quality of arable land. The decline in incomes from rent undoubtedly hastened the break-up of some of the great estates and contributed directly to the diminishing wealth and influence of the old landed aristocracy.

The picture of depression was not reflected across the nation. In the non-arable sectors, such as dairying, meat production, fruit and market gardening, the situation was not as severe. This is apparent when analysing land values across the country. 'In ten counties - Berkshire, Cambridge, Essex, Huntingdon, Kent, Norfolk, Northampton, Oxford, Suffolk, Wiltshire - assessments [rentable value] fell by over 30 per cent between 1879/80 and 1894/5, while in Cheshire and Cornwall the decline was less than 10 per cent in the same period.'[7] It would appear that the depression was regional and largely confined to a specific sector.

b) A 'Quiet Prosperity'

For the farmer involved in mixed husbandry, the pastoral and the market gardening sectors, 'agricultural depression' did not exist. The price falls experienced in the meat sector were by no means as severe as in the arable areas, as the table below makes clear.

Index of Price of Beef and Mutton, 5-Year Averages 1870-1913 (1867-77=100)

	Prime Beef	Prime Mutton
1870-74	102	102
1880-84	99	109
1890-94	80	87
1900-04	85	91
1910-13	91	93

The price falls which did occur were offset by a range of factors which cushioned pastoral and dairy farmers. Particularly important was the growing market for their produce. Furthermore, although there was European competition in certain sectors such as butter and cheese, the more perishable milk sector remained relatively safe from foreign competition. And, although refrigerated meat did begin to reach Britain from the late 1880s, the market remained strong for the domestic product. More people (as the population grew from 26 million in 1871 to 37 million in 1901) and better-off people demonstrated a preference for British-produced meat. Despite a 300 per cent increase in meat imports in the last quarter of the century,

British farmers had maintained a two-thirds share of the market by 1900. Refrigerated New Zealand lamb and American tinned beef provided competition only at the cheaper end of the market. And, despite European competition, British pork, traditionally the poor man's meat, continued to prove profitable. Furthermore, the decline in arable prices assisted the pastoral sector as feed prices fell.

The growth of this and other sectors, such as fruit and market gardening, actually resulted in an overall growth in agricultural incomes during the 'depression' years. Even the arable counties began to show signs of recovery. In reality the depression had removed a good deal of the inefficiency in grain-producing regions. Excessive numbers of labourers had been reduced. The more conservative, scientifically retarded farmers had been forced off the land, and some of the heavier soil areas which were relatively unsuited to grain were no longer cultivated. There were two specific, positive outcomes. First of all, 'inefficient farmers were often replaced by immigrants from other districts who, uninhibited by local traditions which had never been their own, managed to accomplish what had been thought to be against nature. ... Many Scotsmen moved from the grazing districts of their own country to take low rented arable farms in the Midlands or south-east England ... and turn them over mainly to grass.'[8]

Even in those areas where grain production continued, the adoption of technology assisted their survival and ultimate return to profit. The greater diffusion of technical knowledge and the widespread adoption on the larger farms of reaping machines allowed significant wage economies to be made. As the quality of the reaping machines themselves steadily improved, the cost of harvesting fell dramatically, allowing British grain producers to raise incomes. By 1914 the average cost of harvesting wheat had fallen to 3-4 shillings (15-20p) per acre compared to as much as 16 shillings (80p) per acre by hand.

Nevertheless, the image of long-term, general agricultural depression prevailed. This can in part be explained by the nature of the two commissions which publicised the plight of the agricultural industry. The Richmond Commission (1879-82) was dominated by the influence of the landed classes of the arable districts. Almost all the commissioners owned estates in the south-east. Of 35 tenant farmers called as witnesses, only eight were not from this region and sector. Only five witnesses were from the dairy sector. This is perhaps understandable, as those most depressed were inevitably most desperate to be heard. Similarly, although the second Commission of the mid-1890s heard evidence from a broader range of witnesses, and did conclude that problems were not so severe in the pastoral sector, the final report focused very closely on the problems of the arable counties.

By the end of the nineteenth century, Britain had lost any pretence of being a major agrarian nation. Half of the food it consumed came from abroad, the strategic dangers of which were to be felt in the First World War. As industrialisation continued, so agriculture was less important to the economy of Britain. In 1900, 80 per cent of her people were now urban dwellers and agriculture provided only 6.1 per cent of national income, compared to 23 per cent half a century before.

5 Conclusion

a) Relative Decline

The evidence, then, does not support the idea of a great depression. It was, as Mathias claimed, 'a twenty year period of doubts, self questioning and disenchantment.'[9] This is not in itself sufficient to single out the years 1873-96 as a distinct era in its own right. As regards the 'great depression' itself, wrote S.B. Saul, 'surely the outcome of modern research has been to destroy once and for all the idea of the existence of such a period in any unified sense ... the sooner the "great depression" is banished from the literature, the better.'[10]

b) 1896-1914

Historians, having analysed in detail the 1873-96 period, have then to decide whether these years deserve a unique status in British economic history. So controversial and complex was the industrial and economic history of the period that it has overshadowed the following years, up to 1914. We have, in this chapter, seen some of the economic indicators up to 1914, and it is clear that the predominant difference between the two periods relates to price movements. As prices recovered after 1896, with a surge in world demand and the rush of gold discoveries in the United States, South Africa and Australia, so optimism seemed to return to the British industrial sector. Production was stimulated, particularly in Britain's pits. Coal production soared in response to both home and foreign demand: output reached 287 million tons in 1913 compared with around 200 million tons at the turn of the century. For the first time, in 1913, over a million men worked in British coalmines. British shipyards in 1914 built 60 per cent of the world's merchant vessels. A burst of investment in new, bigger cotton mills and much new technology in cotton textiles dragged the Lancashire industry out of the lethargy and conservatism of the past.

Overseas investment too began a relentless rise, adding some £100 million per annum to the value of British foreign assets. London reigned supreme as the world's premier financial centre. The British had, it seemed, even learned something of business organisation with a growth in horizontal integration and the establishment of more powerful companies, for so long apparent in Germany and the

United States. This affected areas as diverse as soap, tobacco, sewing machines, cotton textiles and bleaching.

The end result of this apparent pre-war boom was the boost in the balance of payments account which, having showed a surplus of £40 million in 1900, had grown to £200 million by 1913. And yet the underlying trend remained as it had in 1896. Britain was simply being outperformed by its competitors, increasingly so in the key industrial areas upon which British prosperity hinged. The productivity gap was widening, especially in steel where the German productivity per worker was 80 per cent higher than in Britain. Germany's output dwarfed that of Britain. A similar situation existed in the United States, where productivity was 57 per cent higher and total production more than four times that of Britain.

Little actual change had permeated down to the typical British company, where size and ownership issues had not been resolved. Overall, Britain had failed to develop large industrial corporations, indicating a stubborn resistance to change with the times. Even the British worker had surrendered some of the gains in living standards that had been achieved, as money wages stagnated from 1900 and price rises reduced real wages for many. The fall in real wages was relatively light and did not seriously threaten the improvements of the 1873-96 period. Nevertheless, pressures were sufficient to create tensions in British society. A combination of factors - including a rapid increase in the workforce, as infant mortality rates had slumped from the 1890s - caused the fall in real wages. The growth in the labour force, accompanied by a failure to provide the equivalent number of new jobs, increased pressure on wages. Falling productivity in the coal industry, where workers were paid piece rates (i.e. according to the amount of coal extracted) also contributed to pressure on wages. The alarming rise in industrial disputes, which culminated in a record 41 million working days being lost in 1912, was a direct consequence of such pressures.

Overall then, the years 1873 to 1914 present a complex picture of growth and also of diminishing British domination of the world economy. We can dismiss the idea of a 'great depression', though we must also recognise that the pre-war boom years fail to mark a return to long-term prosperity. The stagnation of the economy in the 1920s and the disastrous economic downturn of genuine depression in the early 1930s present real evidence of Britain's industrial problems. In this respect, the First World War proved to be a watershed in British economic history.

References
1   H.L. Beales, 'The Great Depression in Industry and Trade Economic', *History Review* (Economic History Society, 1934).
2   D.S. Landes, *The Unbound Prometheus* (Cambridge University Press, 1976), p. 336.

3   S.B. Saul, *The Myth of the Great Depression* (Macmillan, 1981), p. 40.
4   M. Sanderson, *The Universities and British Industry* (Routledge, 1972), p. 17.
5   M. Dintenfass, *The Decline of Industrial Britain: 1870-1980* (Routledge, 1992). p. 70.
6   Ibid, p. 21.
7   C. O'Grada In R. Floud and D. McCloskey, *The Economic History of Britain Since 1700*, Vol II (Cambridge University Press, 1981), p. 193.
8   W. Ashworth, *An Economic History of England: 1870-1939* (Methuen, 1969), p. 194.
9   P. Mathias, *The First Industrial Nation* (Methuen, 1969), p. 397.
10 Saul, *Myth of the Great Depression*, p. 54.

Answer essay questions on 'The End of Supremacy, 1873-96'

Consider the following questions:
1.   Summarise the main threats to Britain's economic supremacy as outlined in this chapter.
2.   To what extent, if at all, did the British economy experience a 'great depression' between 1873 and 1896?
3.   Was there a 'great depression' in British agriculture in the later nineteenth century?
4.   To what extent was there a 'failure of entrepreneurship' in British industry in the period from 1873 to 1914?
5.   Analyse the impact of foreign competition on the British economy in the years from 1880 to 1914.

Most essay questions on this period focus on the apparent problems experienced in the economy and the contemporary idea of economic depression. Question 1 simply calls for you to identify the factors which contemporaries and historians have suggested as areas of weakness in the British economy in the last quarter of the nineteenth century. Questions 2-4 follow the same format, one which is generally popular with students, that is the sort of question which requires you to present both sides of the argument before concluding which you find more convincing. Question 2 is clearly the most wide-ranging of the five, requiring you to explore the negative view of economic performance. You should also demonstrate why contemporaries were so pessimistic and where the title 'great depression' originates. Try and avoid listing simple negative and positive points and, instead, get to grips with the issues of relative decline and growing foreign competition whilst production levels and other economic indicators still showed growth.

   Questions 3 and 4 call for the same approach, explaining apparent failure, though concentrating on more specific areas of the economy. Question 5 is more challenging. How can we analyse the impact of competition on the economy? How does the effect of competition manifest itself? Were all areas of the economy equally affected or were there some sectors more seriously damaged by overseas competition? Why did competition emerge from the 1870s and from where? Did Britain have a strategy to deal with competition? Was free trade in any way responsible? Did governments come under pressure to intervene, to aid British industry? What were the long-term implications for Britain's economic future?

Summary Diagram
The End of Supremacy, 1873-1914

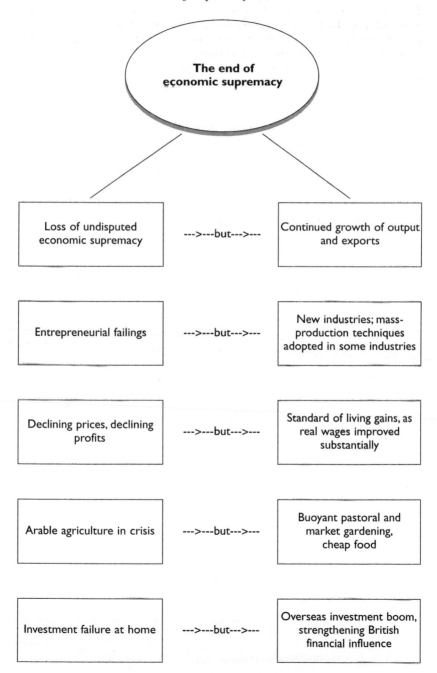

The end of economic supremacy

Loss of undisputed economic supremacy --->---but--->--- Continued growth of output and exports

Entrepreneurial failings --->---but--->--- New industries; mass-production techniques adopted in some industries

Declining prices, declining profits --->---but--->--- Standard of living gains, as real wages improved substantially

Arable agriculture in crisis --->---but--->--- Buoyant pastoral and market gardening, cheap food

Investment failure at home --->---but--->--- Overseas investment boom, strengthening British financial influence

6 Conclusions

In previous chapters we have considered Britain's unique experience in becoming the world's first industrial nation. A rural, agricultural economy had become urban and industrial. In tracing that development, we have now arrived at a crucial point whereby we must assess the impact of industrialisation on the nation and its people. What had been achieved? Had the rise of manufacturing specifically and capitalism generally brought with it tangible gains for the populace? Had the spread of mechanisation reduced the physical demands on labour, or, as Marx claimed, reduced the worker to the status of wage slave, in an increasingly depersonalised workplace dominated by the machine? In other words, had industrialisation been a positive experience?

1 The Creation of Wealth

Assessments of national and personal wealth suggest that a great deal had been achieved over the period covered in this book. In particular, national income (the total value of all goods and services produced by the economy over the course of a year) shows an inexorable rise throughout the nineteenth century, as the diagram below demonstrates.

In terms of industrial expansion, a plethora of data exists, highlighting the astounding increase in production, most notably in the staple industries. We know, for example, that the consumption of raw cotton (the best indicator of overall production levels) was 30 times greater in 1914 than it had been in 1800. Coal production was 24 times greater and iron production 50 times greater over the same

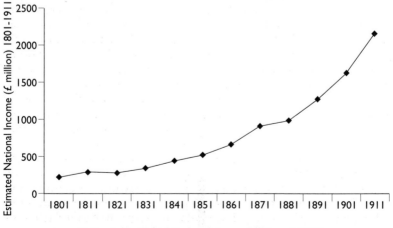

Estimated national income between 1801 and 1911

period. Britain had amassed an empire, which touched every continent and upon which, it was said, the sun never set. The benefits of
economic growth seemed to permeate the whole of British society, as
businesses prospered, millions of jobs were created and incomes
rose. Historians are still locked in uncertainty and debate over the
standard of living debate in the industrial revolution and its immediate aftermath. However, a consensus exists that, generally, living
standards show distinct improvements from the 1850s onwards, as a
result of more stable employment and the boost to real wages as
prices fell from the mid-1870s. In particular, over the final 40 years
of the nineteenth century, real wages rose by an average of 60 per
cent.

The creation of wealth and jobs is tied to the structural changes in
the economy, as 'modern' industry overtook traditional crafts and
agriculture. The relentless rise of manufacturing, mining, trade,
transport and the financial services (see page 10) was responsible for
the increase in national prosperity, transforming the physical appearance of the industrial regions. This also explains the economic and
political fortunes of the middle classes, who, by almost any measure,
were the principal beneficiaries of industrialisation. Accounting for
around a quarter of the population at any given time, the middle
classes became the power brokers of Victorian Britain, dominating
economic activity and extending their political influence at both
national and local levels. Middle-class social attitudes thus exerted
great influence on the social development of the nation.

2 Intervention and Social Improvement

Although *laissez-faire* prevailed as an economic doctrine, it is clear that
the State played a more direct role in the lives of the population from
the 1830s onwards. Even the advocates of economic *laissez-faire* and
the social doctrine of self-help recognised that in some areas only
central-government intervention would suffice. The Poor Law
Amendment Act of 1834 was generally perceived by the poor as a
negative step as, in theory at least, it removed the able-bodied
worker's right to outdoor relief payments. However, the factory acts of
1833 and 1847, and the Mines Act of 1842, were serious attempts at
improving employment conditions. The repeal of the Corn Laws in
1846 was also seen as contributing to the well-being of the 'lower
orders', although repeal was principally for economic motives. Public
health acts in 1848, 1872 and 1875 and other legislation related to
urban conditions also had a material effect on the lives of the people.
The recognition that life in urban Britain had become intolerably
difficult and dangerous touched the guilty conscience of the middle
classes. The last three decades of the nineteenth century witnessed a
rapid expansion of municipal involvement in gas and water schemes.
As important was the expansion of municipal borrowing to finance

sewerage programmes, directly attacking one of the worst aspects of Victorian city life. The widespread provision of municipal cemeteries relieved the pressure on church burial grounds. The enforcement of slum clearance orders and the compulsory provision of modern sanitation in new housing added to the measures which slowly though steadily made inroads into the appallingly high death rates of the mid century. Helped by the rise of real wages, national death rates at last began to fall, especially from the 1880s. Although responding more slowly than general death rates, that key indicator of public health, infant mortality rates (deaths of children in the first year of life) began a rapid decline, falling by one-third between 1900 and 1914.

The extension of the vote to most men through the reform acts of 1867 and 1884 and the compulsory provision of elementary education by 1880 were further examples of the social advances associated with the changing role of the State. Government intervention in the economy may have receded with the advent of free trade, but the wealth generated by industrialisation was at least in part responsible for the State and local authorities playing a more dynamic and constructive role in social change.

For their part, the working classes too contributed to an improvement in their situation. The co-operative movement, Post Office savings, mechanics institutes, trades unions and the temperance movement were, for many, agents of improvement, especially for the more skilled, educated sectors of the working classes. Also, by 1900 an estimated 80 per cent of adult males had some form of sickness cover through friendly society and insurance company schemes.

By 1914, then, the working classes were, on the whole, better fed, better housed and better educated than ever before. The nation possessed enormous wealth, controlled the world's largest empire and was able to provide work for the vast bulk of its ever-growing workforce. The technological advances of the industrialisation period since the last quarter of the eighteenth century had revolutionised industry and communications. And yet, for all this apparent 'progress', Britain by 1914 was not a nation at ease with itself. The changes of the previous 140 years had left in their wake many uncertainties and problems. The industrialisation of Britain had not been an unqualified success.

3 A Legacy of Controversy

From the earliest days of protest surrounding the introduction of new technologies in textiles in the mid eighteenth century to the reassessment of industrial capitalism during the great depression of the 1930s, dissenting voices were heard. Many challenged the belief that industrialisation necessarily meant progress. Some observers presented an idealised interpretation of Britain's pre-industrial past, where work was a more challenging and satisfying experience. In its place, they believed, modern industry had substituted a regime of monotony and exploitation.

a) Useful Work or Useless Toil?

There are certain issues, related to industrialisation, which came under the close scrutiny of contemporary observers. The first of these issues concerns the quality of the work experience. In particular, those of a left-wing persuasion were convinced, as Marx and Engels had claimed in *The Communist Manifesto*, first published in 1848, that:

> 1 Owing to the extensive use of machinery ... the work of the proletarians [the urban, industrial working class] has lost all individual character, and consequently, all charm for the workman. He becomes an appendage of the machine, and it is only the most simple, most monotonous,
> 5 and the most easily acquired knack that is required of him.[1]

Furthermore, critics argued, the machine, whose advanced technology ought to have worked to the benefit of mankind, actually worsened the condition of the worker. The machine '... gifted with the wonderful power of shortening and fructifying [making more productive] human labour, we behold starving and overworking it.'[2]

There was no shortage of support for this point of view. William Morris, intellectual, designer, and leading figure of the early Pre-Raphaelite art movement, denounced what he termed the tyranny of the machine. He, like other influential nineteenth-century intellectuals, not least the great art critic John Ruskin, had been appalled at the relentless advance of industry. Morris, a convert to socialism in 1883, denounced modern industrial practices, developing the 'Arts & Crafts' movement which sought to preserve and extend traditional crafts. His enemy was industrial capitalism. His denunciation of the monotonous toil of the modern worker, highlighted in his article 'Useful Work Versus Useless Toil', promoted the moral value of the work of the skilled craftsman, whose 'worthy work carries with it the ... hope of pleasure in our daily creative skill. All other work is worthless; it is slaves' work - mere toiling to live, that we may live to toil.'[3]

Essentially an idealist, Morris's views harked back 'to an idealised mediaeval world, a Merrie England that existed more in the poetry of Tennyson'[4] than in reality. Herein lies the difficulty with many criticisms of the industrialisation process and the belief that it depersonalised the workplace and diminished the quality of the work experience. Are we to treat such criticism as a valid appraisal of the impact of industrialisation, or the unrealistic, even sentimental opinions of a privileged class? Certainly Carlyle, Marx, Ruskin, Morris and others were distant from the day to day necessity of earning a wage, however aesthetically pleasing or otherwise that work may be. In reality, there had never been a golden age for the labouring classes. Life for most had always been 'nasty, brutish and short'. Was it realistic to hope that modern production techniques could be replaced? Could one dis-invent the machine?

The relative merits of industrialisation have often focussed upon the negative impact on the worker, presenting him or her as the 'victim' of an insidious system that removed all individuality from work. Yet there is a danger of exaggeration. It is clear that not all workers became the slave of the machine. And although working conditions were undoubtedly difficult in many trades, work for many thousands remained an important part of an individual's identity. The novelist D.H. Lawrence, recalling his early life in the coalmining area of Nottinghamshire at the end of the nineteenth century, was able to present a more representative view of the workplace. The son of a coalminer, Lawrence described life as 'a curious cross between industrialism and the old agricultural England. ... The pit did not mechanise men. On the contrary ... the miners worked underground as a sort of intimate community. ... My father loved the pit. He was hurt badly more than once, but he would never stay away.'[5] And so, whilst there is no doubt that the profit motive of capitalism encouraged the use of the most cost-efficient means of production, which might indeed reduce the level of skill required of the worker, it could never completely remove the individuality or identity of the worker.

b) Class Relations

How then did the progress of mechanisation affect the relationship between master and worker? This is a problematic area, for we can only assess the master/worker relationship in the most general manner. There were undoubtedly harsh *and* benevolent employers, but as industrial concerns became larger so the owner actually had no relationship with individual workers. This renders a precise answer impossible. Again, contemporary left-wing opinion was hardly favourable, seeing the middle-class capitalist as a source of conflict and an agent of repression. Employer resistance to trades unionism is often cited as evidence of an oppressive regime, and British trades unions most certainly had to contend with hostile management and indeed government. Strikes were rarely successful since lock-outs (whereby employers refused to allow striking workers to return to work until the employer's terms were accepted), the courts and the dismissal of troublesome individuals proved to be effective weapons until the late nineteenth century.

Low wage levels for the working classes in the face of increasingly opulent middle-class living standards has also been offered as a cause of a declining relationship. As a disproportionate share of increasing national wealth went to the middle classes, so resentment grew. In particular, the apparent unwillingness of the middle classes to recognise and act upon the plight of the poor, created social tension. Friedrich Engels, in denouncing the British capitalist, or bourgeois, claimed in 1844 that 'It is utterly indifferent to the English bourgeois whether his working men starve or not, if only he makes money'.[6] As the middle classes began to desert the towns and cities for the suburbs, so their lives became increasingly remote from the masses. Accusations of ignorance and indifference were frequently heard, as this popular ballad of 1840s Manchester suggests:

1 How little can rich men know of what the poor man feels,
   When want, like some dark demon foe, nearer and nearer steals!
   He never tramped the weary round, a stroke of work to gain,
   And sickened at the dreaded sound telling him 'twas in vain.
5 Footsore, heartsore, he never came back through the winter's wind,
   To a dark cellar, there no flame, no light, no food to find.
   He never saw his children lie shivering, the grass their bed;
   He never heard the maddening cry, 'Daddy, a bit of bread'.

Yet an over emphasis on relationships in larger industrial concerns distorts the overall picture, as more personalised employer/worker relationships did exist in the thousands of small workshops which remained an essential part of the British industrial scene. The changing relationship in the workplace evolved over many years and was subject to great variation from trade to trade and to geographical variations. In any case, the nature of the relationship with one's employer was a secondary consideration for most workers.

c) The Problem of Poverty

The most common source of working-class dissatisfaction remained the grinding poverty that afflicted a great portion of the population. It was this, and the attendant problems associated with poverty, which remained the most pressing social problem of the industrialisation period. Poverty could be caused by any combination of low wages, ill health, unemployment, large families and widowhood. The consequences of poverty, such as poor housing, inadequate diet and ill health often forced the individual or family into a downward spiral. Despite the real wage improvements, across the workforce generally, we are reminded of the dangers of relying too heavily on average figures. Numerous surveys into the lives of the poor demonstrated that severe poverty was endemic in Britain throughout the late eighteenth and the nineteenth centuries. Henry Mayhew's investigation into the lives of the poor in London in 1851, for instance, provided shocking detail on the realities of working-class life. In 1886 the social investigator Charles Booth began a series of inquiries that concluded that 30 per cent of the population of London lived at or below the poverty line. In York, in 1900, Seebohm Rowntree arrived at the same conclusion regarding the poor of that city. The poverty line in both cases was set at a level which covered only the very basics of life, including rent, fuel, clothing and basic nutrition. Low standards may have been expected of London with its serious overcrowding and high proportion of casual workers, but what shocked the readers of Rowntree's report on York was that such standards existed in so small a city without a dense concentration of industry.

In establishing that widespread poverty existed, we are faced with the question of why, in the face of such wealth, the problem was so severe. Had the pursuit of profit ensured that wage levels were low and working conditions poor? Was British capitalism, then, hugely successful in creating wealth, while failing the workers who generated that profit? Had capitalism failed the majority? And yet, from another perspective, had economic growth not generated millions of jobs over the whole period of industrialisation, and in doing so staved off a potentially worse poverty crisis? Furthermore, were low wages not the natural result of growing competition for work in the face of continued population growth?

4 Working-Class Responses

There can be no doubt that industrialisation had a profound effect on the experiences of the working classes, who comprised 70 per cent of the population. The transformation of the nation, through industrialisation, also inevitably elicited a range of working-class responses. What should be noted from the outset is that this sector of the population contained within it a diverse range of people. Distinctive differences existed between skilled and unskilled workers, rural and urban populations, and, of course, the lives of men and women. Similarly, there was no consensus on how to respond to the problems and issues outlined in this chapter. A majority accepted their lives with passivity, even resignation. Others became sporadically involved in protest when personally affected by, for example, unemployment or trades disputes. A small minority existed who possessed a radicalism which might be directed towards political reform and trades union activity.

We can isolate specific points at which such radicalism peaked. Economic distress and protest were often linked. The post-Napoleonic war depression coincided with radical political activity between 1815 and 1822. Rural distress in the late 1820s and 1830s contributed to the Swing Riots and anti-Poor-Law protests. The trade recession of 1837-1842 was the most important period of Chartist protest and saw an upsurge in trades union activity. On the other hand, the high demand for labour and rising living standards of the last quarter of the nineteenth century encouraged greater trades union membership as workers could afford weekly subscriptions. At the same time many workers became more receptive to socialist politics, which inspired a new breed of union leader. Trades union membership increased from 750,000 in 1885 to almost 4 million by 1914.

Poverty, prices, public health, trade recessions and working conditions and many other factors, affected therefore, how the working classes lived and reacted to economic change. For women, the picture is even more complex. What impact did industrialisation have on the role of women? Were the changes positive or negative? Before, and in the early stages of, industrialisation, women arguably played a more equal role to men in both the economy and society generally. Domestic forms of production more easily allowed the woman to combine the roles of worker and mother. The open-field system of agriculture provided a considerable amount of work. Industrialisation brought with it a change in the employment situation of women. The onset of factory production (particularly textile spinning) took women away from the home. Enclosed farms had less work to offer women. Where women did find work, there was clear wage discrimination. Furthermore, although apparently pursued for humanitarian reasons, legislation to protect women in the workplace did not always work in the best interests of them or their families. The factory acts reduced the hours women could work and the 1842 Mines Act disallowed women from working underground and, in doing so, reduced their earnings potential. Increasing social pressures on women to remain in the home after marriage, and the failure to extend the vote to women - despite the three reform acts which extended male suffrage - both helped reinforce the social, political and economic division between the sexes. Despite some improvements in the second half of the nineteenth century, with better access to the professions and legislation to protect and improve a woman's status within marriage, the position of women in British society had arguably worsened in relation to that of men.

5 Assessment

We are left, then, with conflicting views of the exact significance of the industrialisation of Britain between the late eighteenth century and 1914. The pessimists have a good deal of evidence which suggests that the creation of wealth did not bring about 'the greatest good of the greatest number'. Inequality, and an unnecessary level of suffering experienced by the working classes, lie at the heart of their criticisms. Industrial capitalism, they argue, was a repressive force, subjugating one class to the dominance of another. This was done in the pursuit of private profit at the expense of communal well-being.

To the optimists, modernisation of the means of production, more work, improved transport and communication, better access to cheap food, compulsory education and the opening up of the political process are but a few of the tangible benefits of industrialisation. That the nation was transformed is undeniable. The relative merits of that transformation, however, will remain a source of contention. The real significance of 1780-1914 lies, partly, in what it led to. If the sufferings of several generations led their descendants to have fuller, longer lives, unquestionably benefiting from the fruits of technological advance, then we may well see it all as being worthwhile. Alternatively, if the whole world chokes on its own pollution, then industrialisation may well be seen (by alien historians!) as a fatal wrong turning.

References

1   Karl Marx and Friedrich Engels, *The Communist Manifesto* (Penguin, 1985), p.87.
2   J.M. Golby (ed), *Culture and Society in Britain, 1850-1890* (Oxford University Press, 1987),
    p.10.
3   Ibid, p.143.
4   Jonathan Glancey, 'William Morris: A Peculiarly English Socialist', *New Statesman*, May 1996, p.19.
5   Alasdair Clayre (ed), *Nature and Industrialisation* (Oxford University Press, 1977), p. 386.
6   Friedrich Engels, *The Condition of the Working Class in England* (Granada, 1982), p.302.

Chronological Table

1761	Bridgewater Canal opened.
1764	Spinning jenny invented by James Hargreaves.
1769	Water frame invented by Richard Arkwright.
1771	Richard Arkwright and Jedidiah Strutt open the first cotton spinning mill at Cromford, Derbyshire.
1774	Business partnership formed between Matthew Boulton and James Watt, producing a new generation of steam engines.
1776	Adam Smith publishes *Wealth of Nations*.
1779	Samuel Crompton invents spinning mule.
1781	James Watt and William Murdoch develop 'rotary motion', allowing the application of steam power to industrial machinery.
1783	Henry Cort puddling and rolling processes, boosting wrought-iron production.
1785	Edmund Cartwright produces prototype power loom.
1791-94	'Canal mania' investment boom.
1793	Britain becomes involved in Napoleonic wars. Board of Agriculture formed, with Arthur Young as its first Secretary.
1799	Income tax introduced for first time.
1800	Henry Maudsley produces the precision screw-cutting lathe, enhancing precision of machine engineering. Combination Act confirms illegal status of trades unions.
1807	Transport of slaves on British ships illegal. French introduce the *Continental System*, a form of economic warfare, attempting to stop trade to and from Britain. British respond with similar measures against vessels trading with France.
1811-12	Machine-breaking attacks or 'Luddite' protests occur in northern textile districts.
1812	Wheat prices peak at 126 shillings per quarter.
1812-14	War with USA as British navy intercepts American trade with France. Further distress in cotton districts as supply of raw cotton is interrupted.
1815	End of war with France. Corn Laws introduced.
1816-21	Trade recession results in unemployment, poverty and protest. Demands for political reform creates further social unrest.
1817	March of the Blanketeers.
1819	Peterloo massacre. Government passes repressive 'Six Acts' to quell political protest.
1820	Parliamentary Select Committee on Foreign Trade reports in favour of lowering of tariffs.
1823	Significant reduction by government on import duties. Export restrictions on machinery relaxed.
1824	Combination Laws repealed.

1825 Stockton to Darlington Railway opened.

1826 Short trade recession.

1828 Huskisson introduces sliding scale on duty on wheat imports. Neilson develops hot-blast technique for iron furnace.

1830 Opening of Liverpool to Manchester Railway. Trade recession. Rural riots across southern England.

1832 Great Reform Act extends vote to middle-class men.

1833 Factory Act passed.

1834 New Poor Law introduced through Poor Law Amendment Act.

1836-37 Railway investment 'mania'.

1837-42 Most severe economic recession of nineteenth century. Serious economic and social distress, especially 1839-42.

1838 Anti-Corn-Law League founded in Manchester.

1839 Chartist protests begin. First Chartist petition to Parliament defeated. Naysmith's steam hammer introduced for working wrought iron.

1840 Railway investment 'mania'.

1842 Peel's first free-trade budget. Further Chartist disturbances. Second Chartist petition rejected. Mines Act passed.

1844-48 Third railway investment 'mania'.

1845 Peel's second free-trade budget.

1846 Repeal of the Corn Laws.

1847-48 Serious trade recession.

1847 Sharp rise in wheat prices causes food riots. Ten Hours Act passed.

1848 First Public Health Act.

1849-52 Major gold discoveries in California and Australia.

1849 Navigation Laws repealed.

1851 Great Exhibition held in Hyde Park attracts 6.2 million visitors.

1853 Gladstone budget reduces tariffs further.

1856 Bessemer converter introduced, boosting steel production, using non-phosphoric ore.

1858 Trade recession.

1860 Cobden-Chevalier Trade Treaty with France. Gladstone's second tariff-reducing budget.

1861-65 American Civil War disrupts supply of raw cotton. Cotton famine causes distress in cotton-textile districts, especially Lancashire and Lanarkshire.

1867 Second Reform Act increases the electorate. Factory Act and Agricultural Gangs Act extends protection in workplace.

1868 Trades Union Congress formed.

1870-73 Price boom.

1871 Unification of Germany.

1872 Public Health Act splits country into 'Sanitary Areas' and makes appointment of a Medical Officer of Health in each area compulsory.

1873-96 Sustained period of declining prices.

1875 Public Health Act defined public health responsibilities of local authorities.

1879-82 Richmond Commission on state of agriculture.

1879 Gilchrist-Thomas Process allows use of Britain's phosphoric ores in production of cheap steel. Short trade slump.

1880 Mundella's Education Act guarantees compulsory elementary education.

1881 Fair Trade League founded.

1884 Third Reform Act extending the number of men eligible to vote.

1885-87 Short recession and high unemployment. Protests of unemployed in London.

1885-86 Royal Commission on the Depression of Trade and Industry.

1886-90 Overseas investment boom.

1894-98 Royal Commission on Agriculture.

1896 Price falls halted. Red Flag Act suspended, boosting motor industry.

1903 Tariff Reform League founded by Joseph Chamberlain.

1914 Outbreak of the First World War.

Further Reading

A vast amount of material has been published, since the explosion of interest in economic history in the last four decades, dealing with the issue of industrialisation and the nineteenth-century economy. However, a shift towards a more 'econometric' treatment of the subject matter has rendered much of this material inaccessible to those students without prior knowledge of the subject matter. Recommended here are texts which students new to this area of history will find useful. Most of the following also have detailed and helpful bibliographies.

1 General Surveys

One of the most highly regarded studies of the British economy for the 18th to 20th centuries is Peter Mathias, *The First Industrial Nation* (Methuen, 1987), providing a detailed and lucid narrative. More recently, the multi-author texts, *The Economic History of Britain Since 1700*, Vols. I and II (Cambridge University Press, 1994) Roderick Floud and Donald McCloskey (eds), have become classics of their genre. Despite the technical nature of some economic calculations in a few chapters, the texts do provide varied and stimulating analyses of a number of important themes. Essential reading is *Industry and Empire*, by E.J. Hobsbawm (Pelican, 1984), a highly readable and perceptive interpretation of industrialisation in nineteenth-century Britain. For an appreciation of the earlier development of industry and society, students should see John Rule, *The Vital Century* (Longman, 1992), which provides a clear analysis of the nature of England's economic development in the early industrial period, concentrating on 1714-1815. A rather more dense, though worthy, attempt to combine the social and economic forces effecting change in Britain is M.J. Daunton, *Progress and Poverty: An Economic and Social History of Britain, 1700-1850* (Oxford University Press, 1995). Maxine Berg, *The Age of Manufactures: 1700-1820* (Routledge, 1994) is an excellent text dealing also with the nature of early industrialisation. A useful text which helps us understand 19th century industrialisation in its political and social context is Eric J. Evans, *The Forging of the Modern State. Early Industrial Britain 1783-1870* (Longman, 1997). For a more detailed analysis of the economy for particular periods, the most useful texts include, R.A. Church, *The Great Victorian Boom* (Macmillan, 1975), E.J. Hobsbawm, *The Age of Capital, 1848-1875* (Cardinal, 1988), and S.B. Saul, *The Myth of the Great Depression, 1873-1896* (Macmillan, 1969).

2 The Industrial Revolution

Inevitably, as the first industrial nation, Britain's experience has been the focus for the attention of innumerable authors. The starting point for countless historians is the classic historical work, T.S. Ashton, *The Industrial Revolution* (Oxford University Press 1948). Constant revision of our understanding of the origins, nature and impact of the industrial revolution has since produced hundreds of texts. The most useful include, M.W. Flinn, *Origins of the Industrial Revolution* (Longman, 1966), and Phyllis Deane, *The First Industrial Revolution* (Cambridge University Press, 1979). More recently, Pat Hudson, *The Industrial Revolution* (Arnold, 1993) has emerged as a most accessible and interesting synthesis of modern research into the industrial revolution and therefore addresses the historiographical issues that are only briefly referred to in this book. Patrick K. O'Brien and Roland Quinault (eds) have drawn together the economic and social consequences of the industrial revolution in *The Industrial Revolution and British Society* (Cambridge University Press, 1993). Also useful is J. Mokyr (ed), *The British Industrial Revolution: An Economic Perspective* (Westview, 1993). One of the most important texts, although difficult for the inexperienced, is N.F.R. Crafts, *British Economic Growth During the Industrial Revolution* (Oxford University Press, 1985).

3 Transport and Industry

Standard works on transport are many and varied. The best general introduction to the relationship between transport and industrialisation is H.J. Dyos and D.H. Aldcroft, *British Transport and the Economy* (Leicester University Press, 1971). Railways are most effectively dealt with in M.J. Freeman and D.H. Aldcroft (eds), *Transport in Victorian Britain* (Manchester University Press, 1988) and T.R. Gourvish, *Railways and the British Economy, 1830-1914* (Macmillan, 1979). Roy Church, *The History of the British Coal Industry*, Vol. 3 (Oxford University Press, 1986) and B.R. Mitchell, *Economic Development of the British Coal Industry 1800-1914* (Cambridge University Press 1984), provide the most useful works on this particular industry. Cotton-textiles development is clearly outlined in S.D. Chapman, *The Cotton Industry in the Industrial revolution* (Macmillan, 1984) and in rather more detail in D.A. Farnie, *The English Cotton Industry and the World Market* (Clarendon Press, 1979). A good general work on the development of British industry is A.E. Musson, *The Growth of British Industry* (Manchester University Press, 1978). Good on the nation's relative decline is Michael Dintenfass, *The Decline of Industrial Britain 1870-1980* (Routledge, 1992).

4 Agriculture

On the fortunes of agriculture and its links to the economy generally, J.D. Chambers and G.E. Mingay, *The Agricultural Revolution, 1750-1850* (Batsford, 1965) is still informative and relevant despite its age. More recently, a concise analysis is offered by J.V. Beckett, *The*

Agricultural Revolution (Blackwell, 1990). E.J. Jones, *The Development of English Agriculture 1815-1873* (Macmillan, 1974), also provides a pertinent synthesis. The best recent work on agriculture is Mark Overton, *Agricultural Revolution in England* (Cambridge University Press, 1996).

5 Industrialisation and the Working Classes

The recent popularity of social history has resulted in a tidal wave of analysis, interpretation and opinion on the fate of the 'lower orders' in the period of most rapid industrialisation. All students of this period should read Friedrich Engels, *The Condition of the Working Class in England* (Granada, 1982). The classic work by E.P. Thompson, *The Making of the English Working Class* (Penguin, 1980), although now superseded by more recent research, remains a fundamental text. John Rule, *The Labouring Classes in Early Industrial England, 1750-1850* (Longman, 1986) and John Belchem, *Industrialization and the Working Class: The English Experience, 1750-1900* (Scholar Press, 1990), John Benson, *The Working Class in Britain, 1850-1939* (Longman, 1989), also provide superbly written accounts of the experiences and responses of the masses.

Index

A selection of bestselling and related titles from Hodder & Stoughton *Educational*

Title	Author	ISBN	Price (UK)
Labour and Reform:			
Working Class Movements 1815-1914	Clive Behagg	0 340 52930 X	£6.75 ☐
The Growth of Democracy in Britain	Annette Mayer	0 340 69792 X	£6.75 ☐
Poverty and Welfare	Peter Murray	0 340 61891 4	£6.75 ☐
Chartism	Harry Browne	0 340 72070 0	£6.75 ☐
The Changing Role of Women 1815-1914	Paula Bartley	0 340 61135 9	£6.75 ☐

All Hodder & Stoughton *Educational* books are available at your local bookshop, or can be ordered direct from the publisher. Just tick the titles you would like and complete the details below. Prices and availability are subject to change without prior notice.

Buy four books from the selection above and get free postage and packaging. Just send a cheque or postal order made payable to *Bookpoint Limited* to the value of the total cover price of four books. This should be sent to: Hodder & Stoughton *Educational*, 39 Milton Park, Abingdon, Oxon OX14 4TD, UK. EMail address: orders@bookpoint.co.uk. Alternatively, if you wish to buy fewer than four books, the following postage and packaging costs apply:

UK & BFPO: £4.30 for one book; £6.30 for two books; £8.30 for three books. Overseas and Eire: £4.80 for one book; £7.10 for 2 or 3 books (surface mail).

If you would like to pay by credit card, our centre team would be delighted to take your order by telephone. Our direct line (44) 01235 400414 (lines open 9.00am - 6.00pm, Monday to Saturday, with a 24 hour answering service). Alternatively you can send a fax to (44) 01235 400454.

Title _____ First name _____ Surname _____

Address _____

_____

_____

Postcode _____ Daytime telephone no._____

If you would prefer to pay by credit card, please complete:

Please debit my Master Card / Access / Diner's Card / American Express (delete as applicable)

Card number _____

Expiry date _____ Signature _____

If you would not like to receive further information on our products, please tick the box ☐ .